Terror and Transformation

Religion has been responsible for both horrific acts against humanity and some of humanity's most sublime teachings and experiences. How is this possible? From a contemporary psychoanalytic perspective, this book seeks to answer that question in terms of the psychological dynamic of idealization.

At the heart of living religion is the idealization of everyday objects. Such idealizations provide much of the transforming power of religious experience, which is one of the positive contributions of religion to the psychological life. However, idealization can also lead to religious fanaticism, which can be very destructive. Drawing on the work of various contemporary relational theorists within psychoanalysis, this book develops a psychoanalytically informed theory of the transforming and terror-producing effects of religious experience. It discusses the question of whether or not, if idealization is the cause of many of the destructive acts done in the name of religion, there can be vital religion without idealization.

This is the first book to address the nature of religion and its capacity to sponsor both terrorism and transformation in terms of contemporary relational psychoanalytic theory. It will be invaluable to students and practitioners of psychoanalysis, psychotherapy, psychology, and religious studies and to others interested in the role of religion in the lives of individuals and societies.

James W. Jones is Professor of Religion, Adjunct Professor of Clinical Psychology at Rutgers University, New Jersey, and Lecturer in Religion and Psychiatry at Union Theological Seminary in New York. He has doctorates in both clinical psychology and philosophy of religion and has a long history of successful publishing in religious and psychoanalytic subjects.

Terror and Transformation

The Ambiguity of Religion in Psychoanalytic Perspective

James W. Jones

LONDON AND NEW YORK

First published 2002
by Routledge

Published 2002 by Routledge
2 Park Square, Milton Park, Abingdon, Oxon OX14 4RN
711 Third Avenue, New York,NY 10017, USA

Routledge is an imprint of the Taylor & Francis Group, an Informa business

Typeset in Sabon by RefineCatch Limited, Bungay, Suffolk

British Library Cataloguing in Publication Data
A catalogue record for this book is available from the British Library

Library of Congress Cataloging-in-Publication Data
Jones, James William, 1943–
Terror and transformation: the ambiguity of religion in psychoanalytic perspective / James W. Jones.
p. cm.
Includes bibliographical references and index.

1. Psychoanalysis and religion. I. Title.
BF175.4.R44 J657 2002
200'.1'9—dc21

2001037524

ISBN13: 978–1–58391–192–1 (hbk)
ISBN13: 978–1–583–91193–8 (pbk)

For Kathleen

In the last resort we must begin to love in order not to fall ill; and we are bound to fall ill if, in consequence of frustration, we are unable to love.

(Sigmund Freud, 1914: 85)

Religion draws the bow of life so taut that it either snaps the string (defeatism) or overshoots the mark (fanaticism and asceticism) . . . The greater the vitality of religion, the more it may either support or endanger morality. It may create moral sensitivity and destroy moral vigor by the force of the same vitality.

(Reinhold Niebuhr, 1932: 71)

Contents

Acknowledgements

This book began as a paper I was invited to give at a conference at the University of Leiden in October 1998. I want to thank Merteen ter Borg and Hetty Zock for the invitation to come to Leiden and the participants in the seminar, especially Hetty Zock and Rein Nauta, for their comments on that paper. Kate Hawes and her colleagues at Brunner-Routledge made the publishing process a pleasure. As usual, Randy Sorenson went beyond the bounds of friendship and collegiality to read the entire manuscript in rough (very rough) form and provide valuable suggestions and critiques. My approach to the psychology of religion has been made much more nuanced by the many years of ongoing conversation with Naomi Goldenberg, John McDargh, and Diane Jonte-Pace. Even though they would disagree with much that I say in the coming pages, I feel blessed to have friends and colleagues like these. Appropriately this book about love is dedicated to Kathleen Bishop, who, from the first trip to Leiden through the final revision, has companioned me on this journey in ways beyond the power of words to describe or repay.

Introduction

Religion and its ambiguities

In the summer of 1997 I was in Barcelona, Spain, for the European Congress of Psychology of Religion. As part of the conference, our hosts arranged for an excursion high up into the mountains to the shrine of the Virgin of Montserrat, the so-called Black Madonna, the holiest pilgrimage site of the Catalan people. There I joined the long lines of pilgrims winding around the magnificent sixteenth-century basilica, up a narrow stairway, until we came face to face with the small statue of the Virgin Mary, turned black by some unknown process, with Jesus sitting on her lap, holding a small globe that protruded slightly through an opening in the glass enclosure that protected the statue. Pilgrims would touch, kiss, or gently rub that small section of the statue extending through the opening. I was moved by the intensity of their devotion and struck with how physical it was.

After passing the statue myself and returning to the main sanctuary, I noticed an alert-looking young man in his twenties. "Why are you here?" I asked him in simple English. He smiled broadly. "Es very holy here," he said, trying out his English, "Es muy sagrada." It is very sacred. "What does that mean to him?" I wondered as he walked away.

I continued to watch the pilgrims snaking their way towards the shrine. Most were talking intensely on the way up and were quiet and peaceful on the way back. "What prompts them to such intimacies with a painted block of wood?" I wondered. "How would you analyze that psychologically?" I asked myself.

That question was the beginning of this book.

For the last thirty years I have taught religious studies to college students in courses like philosophy of religion, psychology and religion, and religion and science. For the last twenty years I have also worked as a psychotherapist and psychologist in a blue-collar city, in a suburb, in a prison, and in a university. I have also written several books and lectured in different countries on both religion and psychology. In many ways this book, which stands on the boundary of psychology and religion, is a culmination of these many years of teaching, writing, and thinking about the nature of religion and the light psychology might shed on it.

Two questions gave rise to this book: what does it mean to call something sacred as that young man did in the basilica of the Black Madonna? And, how is it that religion has inspired not only great works of art and insightful moral teachings, but also some of our species' most horrific deeds? Can we understand how the same religion can sponsor both terror and transformation?

The first question – What does it mean to call something sacred? – touches one of the major dilemmas in the field of religious studies: What is religion? This is also a question that has become a part of the public conversation. Often I hear people say things like "I am not religious, but I am spiritual." What might they mean? I have wondered. What do they think religion is when they say something like that? So this question of the nature of religion, which I have spent more than thirty years thinking about, is now a topic of discussion among scholars, religious practitioners, and everyday people who stop momentarily to ponder it.

While no-one would dispute that Hinduism and Christianity are religions, I have heard people insist that Buddhism is not a religion. However, they are usually recent North American converts rather than people raised within a Buddhist tradition or scholars of world religions. But they have a point. If we define religion in terms of its content, then it is next to impossible to find a single point accepted by all the traditions that have been called "religious" at one time or another. However, if we define religion by its function, must we then include militantly anti-religious Marxists and Maoists within our scope because such ideologies provide a sense of meaning, create community, or teach values? No wonder most textbooks in the field of religious studies begin with an introductory chapter that contains ample illustrations of this dilemma. One example among many – the text *Exploring Religion* (Schmidt, 1988) – begins with a chapter entitled "What Is Religion" which contains a section called "Problems in Defining Religion."

Recently it has become more common to define religion in terms of the category used by the devotee of the Black Madonna who I met in Spain – "the sacred." Several textbooks use this term in their introductions or even in their titles, for example *The Sacred Quest* (Cunningham et al., 1992) and *Dimensions of the Sacred* (Smart, 1996). However, this only shifts the problem, for we can just as easily ask about the meaning of the term "sacred." On the other hand, without claiming that it is universal or essential, such authors are right to note that designating certain texts, trees, practices, buildings, values, or experiences as "sacred" is a common characteristic of many religious traditions.

If we go further and ask about what it means to call an object, concept, experience, or behavior "sacred," then the psychologist of religion has something to contribute to the discussion. Such is the thesis of this book. Like the term "religion," the category of "psychologist of religion" is also something of an abstraction. There is no generalized psychology of religion. Freudians will address this question rather differently from Jungians, for example. I am neither a Freudian nor a Jungian. I am a professor of religion and a practicing therapist with doctorates in both philosophy of religion and clinical psychology. My own commitments in both my theorizing about religion and my clinical work are informed by a psychoanalytic paradigm that is more relational than Freudian or Jungian in orientation. So what follows will attempt, from within a relational psychoanalytic paradigm, to answer the question of what is involved in calling something "religious," to analyze the psychology behind denoting something as "sacred."

The term "analyze" comes from the Greek word meaning "to loosen" or "to break down into basic components." Like a chemist analyzing water by breaking it down into the elements of hydrogen and oxygen. Freud called his new method "psychoanalysis" – he sought to break an experience or a behavior down to its most basic psychological components. What, we might ask, are the basic psychological components of kissing a statue or calling a place "very sacred"?

The answer to that question depends on the context in which it is asked. What is fundamental about a painting? To the chemist the answer lies in the molecular structure of the pigments on the canvas. To a professor of aesthetics the answer is to be found in the balance, symmetry, harmony, and contrast effects displayed in the work. What are the psychological building-blocks of religious experience?

What are its most fundamental structures? Before answering that we must be clear about the psychological context from which we are speaking.

Psychological theories about the origin and function of religion are often closely tied to a theorist's more general model of human nature. All psychoanalytic theories agree that the individual's manifest character and style, those characteristics that are measured by questionnaires and structured social scientific interviews, are not fundamental. They are the expressions of deeper, more basic psychological forces. Freud, for example, envisioned human nature as a system of antisocial drives that must be channeled, sublimated, or defended against. Within this framework, religion was seen as a way of relating to these drives through repression, projection, and other defenses. Jung thought of human nature as rooted in a transpersonal or collective psychological reality, and for him the function of religion was to give access to that deeper psychological stratum of the personality. Psychological theories of the origin and function of religion, then, carry within them distinctive models of human nature.

In this book I address the question of the psychological building-blocks of religion from within the framework of relational psychoanalytic theory. This relational approach represents a fundamental revision of earlier psychoanalytic views of human nature. Phenomena Freud attributed to biological instincts, the relational theorist sees as the consequence of interpersonal experience. Human relationships are not, as Freud thought, the product of antisocial impulses gradually modified into socially accepted forms out of a compromise between fear and desire. Rather human experience is structured around the establishment and maintenance of connections with others. The nature of these connections – pleasurable, frustrating, or distant – and not their instinctual motivation is what influences the quality of our interpersonal experiences. As W. R. D. Fairbairn said in his typical epigrammatic way, "It is not the libidinal [ie. 'instinctual'] attitude which determines the object-relationship, but the object-relationship which determines the libidinal ['instinctual'] attitude" (Fairbairn, 1952: 34). There is not some free-floating lustful or aggressive instinct bubbling within us. Rather the presence of a seductive or aggressive other evokes these feelings within us. And it is the nature of the relationship and not some impersonal biological drive that determines the quality of the sexual experience. This relational approach is also reflected in D. W.

Winnicott's often-quoted epigram, "There is no such thing as a baby, but only a mother–infant dyad."

For Fairbairn and Winnicott, the self does not develop directly from somatic processes like feeding and cuddling but rather from infant–caregiver interactions. If these instinct-driven episodes carry sufficient parental attunement they contribute to positive self formation. Their psychological import comes not from their instinctual energy but from the meaning they acquire in the context of early interpersonal encounters. It is no exaggeration to say, as Greenberg and Mitchell do, that "the change in theoretical principles of motivation that Fairbairn is proposing is not trivial; it provides a different conceptual framework for viewing the entirety of human experience" (Greenberg and Mitchell, 1983: 156). Such a view conceives of the building-blocks of personality neither as biological drives and defenses against them nor as universal archetypal forms but rather as the internalization of relational episodes laid down in the course of our development. These relational themes echo and re-echo through our devotional practices, spiritual disciplines, cherished philosophical and theological convictions, and our states of ecstasy (Jones, 1991).

The attribution of sacrality takes place in a relational context. There is the relationship of the devotee to whatever object, concept, or experience she calls sacred. To kiss a statue, to be inspired by a text, to be committed to meditating every day, to reverently receive the Holy Communion, is to maintain a special relationship with these objects of devotion. Beyond that the devotee brings a whole history of relational experiences to every encounter with what he names as sacred. Such a history of interpersonal experiences shapes, forms, and (if all is not well) deforms us. Such a relational history resonates in the gods we denounce or embrace, the texts that inspire or bore us, the ideals that compel our assent or revulsion. The relational experiences we have internalized, been moved by, and been stricken with are the precursors that make it possible (or impossible) for us to denote things as sacred and that shape the contours of that affirmation (or lack of it).

So I agree with those who say the construct of the "sacred" is at the core of much of what we call religion. The thesis of this book is that idealization is a major psychological dynamic implicated in experiencing or denoting a text, an institution, a teaching, or a tree as sacred. Idealization is central to the religious life: to be religious is, among other things, to idealize something or someone. To call something or someone sacred is, in part, to idealize them. In addition I will argue that understanding the dynamic of idealization helps account for the ambiguity that has characterized the history of every major religion: that religion can be a source of great good – inspiring people to tremendous acts of self-sacrifice and producing powerful, positive changes in people's lives – and the motivation for horrific individual and collective acts against humanity.

The first chapter begins by illustrating my claim about the role of idealization with some examples from a variety of religious traditions and suggests a parallel here with romantic love. It explores the psychodynamics of idealization by comparing the psychoanalytic theories of Sigmund Freud and Heinz Kohut with particular attention to their approaches to understanding religion. In the psychoanalytic literature, the term idealization covers a variety of phenomena. For Freud idealization is derived from what he calls primary narcissism – the energy with which the child loves itself. The child can also invest some of this self-love in another, seeing the other as simply an extension of itself. For Freud maturity involves journeying from this primary narcissism to "object love" – seeing the other realistically as an independent object and outgrowing one's narcissistic wishes for bliss, merger, and the idealization of self or other. Any traces of the earlier state of primary narcissism with its idealization of an other – say in religious belief or romantic love – represent failures of development and the persistence of an infantile way of relating to the world.

For Kohut, on the other hand, narcissism is not simply an infantile state to be outgrown but is, also, the source of self-esteem, vitality, goals, and ambitions. Thus narcissism and its concomitant need for objects of idealization and sources of self-esteem cannot simply be put aside but must be transformed from immature to mature forms. In his critique of religion, Freud connects religion to infantile narcissism and narcissism's drive for idealization. Because of this, for him religious belief is always a mark of immaturity. Given the connection between narcissism, idealization, and religion, a re-evaluation of the role of narcissism and idealization, as carried out by Kohut, will have important implications for a revamped psychoanalytic understanding of religion.

Having laid out the psychodynamics of idealization, the second chapter portrays some of these dynamics through the presentation of two case studies. While only one of these cases deals directly with religion, together they illustrate some of the forms of narcissism and idealization that are often seen in religious believers and anti-religious partisans. Chapter 3 returns to the main argument concerning the nature of religion and the role of idealization and points out some of the connections between the dynamic of idealization and the experience of the sacred. Many theorists of the sacred define it by its opposition to the profane. Two nineteenth-century scholars of religion, Emile Durkheim and Rudolph Otto, are discussed in some depth as classic examples of this approach. The perspective of contemporary relational psychoanalysis – especially the work of Fairbairn, Winnicott, and Kohut – is shown to generate a rather different perspective on the experience of the sacred from that of Durkheim and Otto.

As part of this discussion, a psychological analysis is offered of Durkheim's and Otto's polarizing of the sacred and the profane. This discussion exposes the ambiguity of idealization in religion: idealization is a crucial agent in the transforming power of religious experience and it is also a means by which religious devotees are kept infantilized and religious fanaticism is strengthened.

To expose these connections between idealization and religious authoritarianism and fanaticism and the terrors they create, the fourth chapter surveys a variety of material: Fairbairn's ideas about what he calls the "moral defense" against bad object relations, Melanie Klein's theory of splitting, clinical reports of religious patients, and social-scientific research into correlations between religion and various personality factors. In the psychology of religion, Kohut's theories have often been deployed in a purely descriptive sense, putting aside the powerful critique of religion that characterized Freudian and classical psychoanalytic approaches to religion. In the past I have been accused of this overly friendly and insufficiently critical approach myself (Miller-McLemore, 1999; Jonte-Pace, 1999). Chapter 4 will argue that an analysis of religion that uses Kohut's theories must be critical and not simply descriptive.

Chapter 5 explores in more detail the possible connections between idealization and the transforming power of religious experience. Drawing on the work of Winnicott, Loewald, Bollas, and other contemporary relational theorists within psychoanalysis, this chapter develops a psychoanalytically informed theory of the transforming effect of encounters with sacred realities.

Given the ambivalent nature of religious idealizations – their transforming power and their problematic connection to religious authoritarianism and fanaticism – the sixth chapter wonders whether or not there can be religion without idealization. The fourteenth-century text *The Cloud of Unknowing*, will be discussed in some depth in order to explore one possibility for a de-idealizing religious practice. Classical psychoanalysis (represented by Freud and his early followers) often linked the de-idealizing of religion to becoming disillusioned with it. De-idealizing religion went hand in hand with abandoning it. This chapter will suggest that de-idealization may also coincide with new forms of religious practice.

While utilizing psychoanalytic theory and social-scientific research, the argument of this book is conducted primarily through the employment of examples and illustrations. It opens with examples from a variety of religious traditions of what I mean by "idealization." These examples are chosen because they are from different religious, cultural, and historical periods. Yet I think they bear what the philosopher Wittgenstein called a "family resemblance" to each other in terms of the dynamic of idealization. Then the second chapter presents two case studies, again with the purpose of illustrating the psychodynamic processes under discussion here. This approach is very much in keeping with my own training. Like most psychoanalytically informed, practicing clinicians, for me the case study is the major vehicle of presenting one's ideas.

As someone who regularly attends meetings both of clinicians and of philosophers of religion, I have often remarked that the clinicians insert a case study everywhere a philosopher would want a formal argument, and vice-versa. The use of case studies here should alert the reader whose primarily mode of discourse is formal argumentation or statistical analysis that while some of both will be employed here, the primary mode of presentation is more like a clinical discussion of cases. While drawing on classical texts in the field of psychology of religion by Freud, Fromm, Allport, and others as well as empirical studies, the claim that idealization is central to the religious life and is connected to authoritarianism and fanaticism is buttressed primarily by many examples from different traditions. And the development of a psychoanalytic account of the transforming power of encounters with sacred realities in Chapter 5 begins from two accounts – one from Pentecostal Christianity, the other from Tibetan Buddhism – of such experiences. The choice of these two examples is far from random since I have spent time among various Pentecostal and charismatic groups and also studied Tibetan Buddhism. And the suggestion in the final chapter that religion can be de-idealizing as well as idealizing also proceeds by recounting various examples from the history of religion. So whether or not readers are convinced by the book's argument concerning the centrality and ambiguity of idealization in religion depends in part on whether or not they share the author's conviction that relational psychoanalytic theory can provide some interpretative gain in understanding religion and also whether or not they are convinced by the relevance of the examples and illustrations.

Every author has fantasies about who will read his or her book. This is especially true of someone like myself who has written books both for professional colleagues and for a wider audience. Since the question "What is religion?" and the dangers of religious fanaticism are of concern both to professionals like scholars of religion or psychotherapists as well as to members of the general public, it is my fantasy that both might read and profit from this book. My (perhaps naive) wish is that this book contains enough technical material and original discussion to appeal to professionals and that is written in a way that is clear and compelling enough to interest a wider audience.

Chapter 1

Religion and idealization

We begin with the question of what is religion. One characteristic of virtually all religions was pointed out by the young man I met in the basilica in Spain who said that the statue he had just kissed was "very sacred." Almost every religion has a person or persons, a text or texts, a ritual or meditative practice, a tree or mountain or statue, that its adherents consider "very sacred." To be religious is, in part, to be devoted to something that is experienced as sacred or holy.

Consider five texts from four religious traditions.

> All the faithful of Christ must believe that the holy and Apostolic See and the Roman Pontiff possesses the primacy over the whole world, and that the Roman Pontiff . . . is the true vicar of Christ and the head of the whole church and the father and teacher of all Christians and that the full power was given to him in blessed Peter to rule, feed, and govern the universal church. Hence we teach and declare that by the appointment of our Lord the Roman Church possesses a superiority of ordinary power over all other churches and that this power of jurisdiction of the Roman Pontiff . . . is immediate; to which all of whatever rite or dignity, both individually and collectively are bound by their duty of hierarchical subordination and true obedience, to submit not only in matters which belong to faith and morals, but also to those that appertain to the discipline and governance of the church throughout the world . . . this is the teaching of Catholic truth from which no one can deviate without loss of faith and salvation . . . we teach and define that the Roman Pontiff . . . is possessed of that infallibility with which the divine Redeemer willed that his Church should be endowed . . . and that therefore such definitions of the Roman

Pontiff are irreformable of themselves . . . But if anyone . . . presume to contradict this our definition: let him be anathema.
(Dogmatic Decree of Pope Pius IX, 1870)

The Bodhisattva, bound to Transcendent Wisdom, lives with nothing clouding his mind. Lacking confusion, he is intrepid, and having passed beyond error, reaches nirvana. All Buddhas, of the past, present, or future, bound to irrefutable Transcendent Wisdom, reach completely full understanding and the highest awakening. Therefore Transcendent Wisdom should be known as the great mantra, the great knowledge mantra, the invincible mantra, the unsurpassable mantra, causing all suffering to cease. It is trustworthy because it is not in error.
(from the *Heart Sutra*)

It is the basic tenet of Judaism that the Torah, in its entirety with interpretations and rules of exegesis and codification was divinely given. It is unchangeable.
(quoted in Selengut, 1994: 250)

All those Boddhisattvas who in this assembly have heard well only a single stanza, a single verse, or who even by a single rising thought have joyfully accepted this Sutra, to all of them . . . I predict their destiny to supreme and perfect enlightenment . . . whoever shall hear this and after hearing, if only a single stanza, joyfully accept it, even with a single rising thought . . . I predict their destiny to supreme and perfect enlightenment.
(from the *Lotus Sutra*)

For you alone are the Holy One
you alone are the Lord
you alone are the Most High,
Jesus Christ
(from the Gloria from the new
Episcopal liturgy)

Psychologically, what do these passages from different traditions – all of which evoke something sacred – have in common? One common theme is the dynamic of idealization; all idealize something. The first idealizes an institution – the Roman Catholic Church and its Papacy – as infallible and worthy of unquestioning obedience. The second idealizes a practice – reciting a mantra – as producing perfect Wisdom. The third idealizes a text. The fourth also idealizes a text which it says is so powerful that even a single verse is able to produce complete enlightenment. The last idealizes a Messianic figure as the only Lord and the only Holy Being. This dynamic of idealization is one, but certainly not the only, fundamental psychological element in the encounter with some object or experience that is considered sacred.

In this way religious experience parallels the experience of romantic love. In both cases some other, some object, is seen in idealized terms. Consider one of the earliest love poems in Western literature, the Song of Songs,

> How beautiful are your sandalled feet . . .
> The curves of your thighs are like jewels,
> the work of a skilled craftsman . . .
> Your breasts are like twin fawns
> two fawns of a gazelle.
> Your neck is like a tower of ivory . . .
> How beautiful, how entrancing you are
> my loved one, daughter of delights.
> You are stately as a palm tree
> and your breasts are the clusters of dates.
> I said I will climb up the palm to grasp its leaves.
> May I find your breasts like clusters of grapes on the vine,
> the scent of your breath like apricots
> and your whispers like spiced wine . . .
> You are beautiful dearest . . .
> Turn your eyes away from me
> they dazzle me . . .
> There may be sixty princesses,
> eighty concubines, and young women beyond counting,
> but there is one alone, my dove, my perfect one . . .
> Who is this that looks out like the dawn,
> beautiful as the moon, bright as the sun
> majestic as the starry heavens . . .?
> I did not know myself;
> she made me feel more than a prince
> reigning over the myriads of his people.
> (Song of Songs 7:1–9; 6:4–12, NEB, slightly altered)

Partly because they have in common this psychological dynamic of idealization, religions have often used the imagery of love, and even romance and sexuality, to convey their most intense experiences. Under the inspiration of the Song of Songs, St John of the Cross wrote one of his most profound descriptions of mystical ecstasy, which contains erotic stanzas such as,

> The Bride has entered
> Into the pleasant garden of her desire,
> And at her pleasure rests,
> Her neck reclining on the gentle arms of the Beloved.

This, John says, describes the soul's being betrothed to God and resting only on the power of the Almighty (St John of the Cross, 1961).

Evangelical Christians regularly sing of the love of Jesus in hymns that shout, "What wondrous love is this," or speak of "Love divine, all loves excelling." They exclaim, "How sweet is His love to me" and sing of the "Love that will not let me go." Evangelicals want to "Tell the sweet story of love" and call for "More love to thee O Christ, more love to thee."

In India the worshippers of Kali, like the nineteenth-century Bengali mystic Ramakrishna, picture the goddess as "the perfect erotic object" – naked with ample breasts and shapely thighs in a seductive pose – and worship her with sensual music and dance and a mantra which contains images of lust, fire, and sexual desire (Kripal, 1998: 89).

It is not coincidence that religious devotees write poems, sing songs, and use language that often parallels the secular language of romantic love. Deep psychological connections are at work here, including the dynamic of idealization. The beloved – whether that be the bride of the Song of Songs, Ramakrishna's Kali, the latest woman in the life of any popular rock and roll singer, the Jesus of evangelical devotion – is inevitably idealized.

Ecstatic experience – whether in the honeymoon suite or the Pentecostal meeting hall – involves more than the release of emotion; it also involves an idealized object. Such ecstasies demand letting go of inhibitions and giving oneself over to another and to the powerful psychological currents that are thereby set free. And, as we shall see, one can only abandon oneself so completely, so unreservedly, to another who is highly idealized. So idealization becomes an important dynamic in many religious texts and practices, since devotion requires idealization, and it is also a crucial catalyst for the transforming ecstasies of the encounter with sacred objects.

FREUD ON LOVE AND IDEALIZATION

One of the first to describe the dynamics of idealization was Sigmund Freud in his essay "On Narcissism" (1914), in which he discusses the dynamic of idealization in terms of what he calls "primary narcissism." Primary narcissism refers to the way in which the infant loves itself and feels itself to be the center of the universe. In the process of loving another, the child (or the childish adult) projects a portion of this primary narcissism onto the beloved, seeing them as perfect and complete. This projection depletes the infant (or the adult) of a portion of its primary narcissism. Thus for Freud, there is always a trade-off between idealization and self-esteem. Idealization comes at a cost to self-love and self-affirmation. Since the amount of energy available is limited, if it is given to the beloved, it is taken from oneself.

> Libidinal object-cathexis does not raise self-regard. The effect of dependence upon the love-object is to lower that feeling . . . A person who loves has, so to speak, forfeited a part of his narcissism and it can only be replaced by his being loved.
>
> (Freud, 1914: 98)

For Freud, love and idealization walk hand in hand. He writes,

> Being in love consists in a flowing-over of ego-libido on to the object. It has the power to remove repressions and re-instate perversions. It exalts the sexual object into the sexual ideal . . . [since] being in love occurs in virtue of the fulfillment of infantile conditions for loving, we may say that whatever fulfills that condition is idealized.
>
> (Freud, 1914: 100)

Since it involves an "overvaluation," romantic love, with its idealization, involves a break with reality-testing and so is always immature and dangerous. Attachment to a love-object, Freud writes

> displays the marked sexual overvaluation which is doubtless derived from the child's original narcissism and thus corresponds to a transference of that narcissism to the sexual object. This sexual overvaluation is the origin of that peculiar state of being in love, a state suggestive of a neurotic compulsion, which is thus traceable to an impoverishment of the ego as regards libido in favor of the love-object.
>
> (Freud, 1914: 88)

Such an "impoverishment of the ego" is too costly for Freud. Maturity involves a journey from this primary narcissism to embracing the reality principle in which the other is seen objectively and realistically and such idealizations are left behind. The reality principle is subverted by the power of narcissistic wishes when either the self or a beloved other are granted powers and qualities beyond what is realistic.

In the course of normal development, according to Freud, the inevitable intrusions of reality gradually undercut the infant's narcissism, eventually leading to the acceptance of the objective world. Narcissistic libido is thereby transformed into "object libido" in which the child ceases to experience reality as an extension of her infantile grandiosity. Proper development journeys from primary process to secondary process, outgrowing the pleasure principle and embracing the reality principle. The illusory and the infantile are gradually brought under the control of the real and the rational. Any remaining infantile illusions are a continuation of a primitive mental state and so represent the greatest danger to rationality and sanity. Such claims involve a retreat from reality into the seductive and gratifying but ultimately destructive world of illusion.

If the reality principle is weak, one is left vulnerable to what Freud calls "a cure by love" which the neurotic, Freud writes sarcastically, "generally prefers to a cure by analysis" (1914: 101). While such a "cure" may be transformative, "it bring[s] with it all the dangers of a crippling dependence" (1914: 101). Psychoanalysis is not, for Freud, a cure through love. Or, more precisely, the love which Freud speaks about as a bulwark against illness is not romantic love with its extravagant idealizations (like those spilling forth from the Song of Songs) but rather, as Stephen Mitchell describes it, it is "realistic love tempered by secondary-process [which] often seems a sober dispassionate affair" (Mitchell, 1997: 24).

This sharp dichotomy between primary narcissism, which brings with it inevitable idealizations and dependencies, and the reality principle informs Freud's analysis of religion in *The Future of an Illusion*. Illusions are defined by their appeal to infantile narcissism and to the wishes and fantasies it generates. "Not necessarily false," rather "we call a belief an illusion when wish-fulfillment is a prominent factor" (1964: 49). The three functions which he ascribes to religion are all "derived from human wishes" (1964: 48).

First, civilization is a dominant source of human misery because of its imposition of instinctual controls. The rational person accepts this misery as the price paid for the advantages of culture. The immature demands to be rewarded in the imaginary, heavenly realm of eternal, narcissistic bliss that religion supplies. Second, science shows us that nature is impersonal, mechanical, uncaring. The adult accepts these objective facts and learns to live with the reality that his or her life, like all of nature, is meaningless and purposeless. The infantile flee from this assault on their narcissism into the illusion that a warm and caring God stands behind the impersonal façade of nature. Third, the greatest cruelty of fate is the finality of death. The realistic and rational person resigns him- or herself to life's transitoriness. The narcissistically inclined cannot accept that life is temporary and so cling to the illusion of life after death. Religion, then, appeals to and reinforces our narcissistic inclinations. Religious claims cannot be "precipitates of experience or end results of thinking" but can only represent "fulfillments of the oldest, strongest, and most urgent wishes of mankind" (Freud, 1964: 47).

For Freud there was no middle ground between primary narcissism and the reality principle. Science was the bearer of the reality principle and so anything outside the ken of science was quickly assigned to the domain of narcissism and rejected on that account alone. For example, writing about claims to foretell the future, Freud says that such a claim "corresponds too closely to certain ancient and familiar human desires which criticism must reject as unjustifiable pretensions" (quoted in Merkur, 1992). Anything remotely analogous to primary narcissism must, of necessity, be discredited. No leniency is allowed when it comes to infantile wishes. Even more liberal or intellectual religious beliefs are impossible "so long as they try to preserve anything of the consolation of religion" (Freud, 1964: 89). Any hint of consolation must be denied.

Besides wish-fulfillment, another aspect of narcissism, which enters into Freud's discussion of religion, is dependency. Freud continually draws a connection between objects of idealization and objects of dependency. This starts with the idealized father on whom the child is absolutely dependent. Again, if childish mental attitudes are not outgrown, the individual continues to look for an object to carry this need for idealization and dependency. In adulthood, of course, the parental figure will no longer do. Something of this need to idealize may be carried over into the experience of romantic love, in which (as we have seen) the beloved is idealized and autonomy and self-esteem are thereby forfeited and the individual becomes, in Freud's eyes, neurotically dependent on the other.

For Freud, a more direct line can be drawn from the child's dependency on his father to the worship of, and dependency upon, God.

> The derivation of religious needs from the infant's helplessness and the longing for the father aroused by it seems to me incontrovertible . . . I cannot think of any need in childhood as strong as the need for a father's protection . . . The origins of the religious attitude can be traced back in clear outlines as far as the feeling of infantile helplessness.
>
> (1962: 19)

The narcissistic elements in religion trouble Freud the most: its keeping adults in a state of infantile dependency and its denial of reality, especially by promises of consolation that mitigate the harsh truths about life discovered by the sciences, and its pandering to the infantile, narcissistic wish to feel special and live forever.

For Freud, religion consists entirely of these narcissistic, infantile wishes and dependencies. He writes of religion,

> Only such a being ["an enormously exalted father"] can understand the needs of the children of men and be softened by their prayers and be placated by the signs of their remorse. The whole thing is so patently infantile, so foreign to reality, that to anyone with a friendly attitude to humanity it is painful to think that the great majority of mortals will never be able to rise above this view of life.
>
> (1962: 21)

Thus Freud was in no position to wonder if there could be a vital religion that was not simply derived from infantile narcissism. For Freud all neurotics, including religious devotees, are completely in the grip of infantile fantasies. Since acceptance of the reality principle is the sole criterion for mental health, there is no place for any accounts of religious motivation or its role in human development other than those that treat religion as infantile and neurotic.

In the past I have been critical, some have said too critical (Jonte-Pace, 1999; Miller-McLemore, 1999), of Freud for framing his argument against religion within an epistemologically much too narrow definition of reality (Jones, 1996). In some ways my criticism is anachronistic since the definition of reality Freud uses in contrasting the reality principle with the claims of religion is the one dominant in his age, derived from Newtonian physics, Victorian biology, and positivistic philosophy. It is no criticism of Freud to say that he lived before the advent of a far more complex physics and more pluralistic philosophy of science. His captivity to a nineteenth-century Darwinian model of human nature and Newtonian definition of science did compromise the universality he wished for in his critique of religion. However, I agree that Freud's critique remains valid to the extent that a religion plays upon infantile forms of narcissism, encourages childish dependency, demands the denial of reality, or promotes untempered idealizations.

KOHUT ON NARCISSISM AND IDEALIZATION

In his explorations of narcissistic disorders and the vicissitudes of narcissism, Heinz Kohut elaborated the developmental trajectory of idealization in great detail. Like Freud, he begins theorizing from an infant in a state of primary narcissism. This idyllic world is inevitably disturbed by lapses in parental care – the breast is not always there on command, the diaper takes too long to be changed, a hug is not always forthcoming at the exact moment of discomfort. To keep the cherished narcissistic experience alive, Kohut suggests that the child creates two internal realities that continue to carry that experience: a grandiose image of the self; and an idealized image of the parent in which the child gives over "the previous perfection to an admired, omnipotent (transitional) self-object: the idealized parent imago" (Kohut, 1971: 24). Thus the propositions "I am perfect" and "You are perfect but I am a part of you" are "the two basic narcissistic configurations" and they serve to "preserve a part of the original experience of narcissistic perfection" (Kohut, 1971: 27).

In order to hold onto that early experience of narcissistic bliss as long as possible, the developing child needs these two idealizations – of itself and its parents. But, since the perfection of the early narcissistic state cannot last, the child also needs these idealizations to fail. But these idealizations need to fail in a special way. Hopefully the child will experience gradual, not sudden or traumatic, disappointments in the idealized parents or his idealized view of himself. Thus the child's view of her parents or herself will gradually become more and more realistic over time. This graded process of disappointment and increasingly realistic assessment leads, Kohut argues, to the internalization of the psychological capacities that the parents previously provided. For example, the experience of being joined to an idealized parent gradually becomes internalized as the capacity to choose one's own values and goals and commit oneself to them. Feeling connected to a greater, ideal reality is no longer dependent on the presence of an idealized parental figure. Through this internalization, the developing person gains a measure of autonomy. She no longer needs to depend on an idealized parent (or parent figure) but can choose her own ideals to which to commit herself.

"Transmuting internalization" is the name Kohut gives to this process by which the idealizations of the parents and one's self are gradually replaced by a more realistic assessment and the child assumes responsibility for the psychological functions previously provided by the idealization of the parents and their reinforcing the child's narcissism. This process of "transmuting internalization" is the key to Kohut's model of development in which experiences with external objects become "transmuted" into what Kohut calls "psychic structures," that is certain psychological capacities and abilities. The child begins by idealizing the parent and creating a grandiose image of herself. But these idealized and grandiose images of parents and one's self, carriers of the early state of primary narcissism, are open to correction and modification through actual experience. The gradual awareness of the parent's shortcomings and the limits of one's own grandiosity transform the experience of idealizing the parents into the ability to choose values and make commitments, and the need for constant admiration from others becomes transmuted into a healthy and realistic sense of self-esteem (Kohut, 1971: 40–41).

If, at an early age, the child experiences a severe or sudden loss of the idealized parent through their disappearance from the child's life or a shattering disappointment in the parent, then this gradual process of internalization cannot happen. The child does not develop his own internal capacity to choose and commit himself to values and goals. Instead, even as an adult, he remains totally dependent on external objects to provide that necessary sense of connection to something of value and to buttress his self-esteem. Remaining in this state of infantile dependency leaves the person in a condition Kohut calls, in a telling phrase, "object hunger," which he describes as follows:

> The intensity of the search for and of the dependency on these objects is due to the fact that they are striven for as a substitute for the missing segments of the psychic structure. They are not objects (in the psychological sense of the term) since they are not loved or admired for their attributes, and the actual features of their personalities, and their actions, are only dimly recognized. They are not longed for but are needed in order to replace the functions of a segment of the mental apparatus which had not been established in childhood.
>
> (1971: 45)

If development goes well, interpersonal experiences are transformed into the structures that give the personality a relative sense of coherence and independence. If development goes poorly and those "self structures" do not develop, the individual is left pathologically dependent on and desperately hungry for external objects to provide the ideals he needs and to buttress his fragile sense of self-esteem.

Trauma, then, results in a "developmental arrest" in which the formation of "self structures" like the capacity to commit oneself to ideals and goals or a healthy and realistic self-esteem fails to take place. These missing psychological capacities must be made up for by a desperate dependency on external agents. However, if a therapist or other caring person provides just the right balance of narcissistic supplies (like support and affirmation) and an "optimal frustration," the process of development can begin again. Transmuting internalization can finally take place in which the idealization of the therapist and the therapist's acceptance of the patient's narcissism can be transmuted into self structures like the capacity to choose or realistic self-esteem that failed to develop earlier.

For Freud, idealization and grandiosity were the antagonists of realism and reality-testing; for Kohut, there is a reciprocal relationship between them. Narcissistic drives and reality-testing work together developmentally, not only in childhood but also throughout life. Rather than renouncing the former and trying to live wholly out of the latter, Kohut champions a continual dialectic between them. Every vital activity requires a balance between narcissistic energy and reality-testing – a balance that is sought but never completely achieved. Narcissistic, idealizing connections are necessary for us to be emotionally invested in a person or an activity. Reality testing is necessary to keep our narcissistic drives grounded in reality and to keep the expectations spawned by them realistic. This dialectic is expressed very clearly in Kohut's description of romance, so different in tone from Freud's:

> the overestimation of the object with which one is in love is indeed a function of the narcissistic libido which is amalgamated with the object cathexes . . . the narcissistic component of a normal state of being in love . . . does not detach itself from the object cathexes but remains subordinated to them and does not – with the single exception of the moderately unrealistic overestimation of the object – lose touch with the realistic features of the object . . . The lover does not lose touch with reality – again with the exception of the moderately unrealistic overestimation of the love object – despite the fact that his creative activity is nourished by narcissistic-idealizing libido.
>
> (Kohut, 1971: 76)

Rather than simply renouncing idealization, Kohut is calling for a much more complex strategy in which one is both deeply emotionally invested in the other and also realistic in one's assessment of them. He is not calling for love without idealization but rather love in which idealization and realism coexist in tension. In the final chapter we will discuss how this same dialectic might apply to religion.

For Kohut, the idealization of one's self and the idealization of a parent or other caregiver are the two major vehicles for the normal development of a healthy sense of self. Later he added a third called the twinship experience. Whereas for Freud, narcissism and idealization are at best necessary components of the infantile period, to be outgrown as soon as possible, for Kohut the narcissistic requirements of self-love and self-cohesion remain throughout life. Throughout the life-cycle, the self remains in relation to others that support and reinforce its needs for objects of idealization as well as mirroring its sense of self. Such objects, which the self needs to sustain its sense of coherence and vitality, are called by Kohut "selfobjects." Selfobjects are the people, places, and things that maintain and enhance an individual's self-esteem, creativity, and self-efficacy and in which the individual can invest her energies. What Kohut calls the selfobject transferences of idealizing and mirroring (and twinship) are three vectors of that emotional investment: towards objects of idealization, towards objects which reflect back to us our achievements and successes, towards objects which ratify a sense of belonging.

These three experiences – idealizing, mirroring, and twinship – are necessary for a cohesive sense of self, the *sine qua non* for Kohut of mental health. This self-cohesion is expressed in what Kohut calls the self's "nuclear program," a core set of authentic goals and ambitions the pursuit of which gives life zest and vitality. Without this deeply rooted sense of direction, the person feels empty and lost and easily falls prey to depression or various forms of borderline character pathology.

Idealization, as a central component of narcissism, remains important throughout the life-cycle. Kohut writes:

> Idealizing narcissistic libido not only plays a significant role in mature object relationships, where it is amalgamated with true object libido, but it is also the main source of libidinal fuel for some of the socioculturally important activities which are subsumed under the term creativity, and it forms a component of that highly esteemed human attitude to which we refer as wisdom.
>
> (Kohut, 1971: 40)

Maturity does not mean leaving narcissism behind.

Kohut recognizes that idealization is central to religious experience. He traces the experience of religious inspiration to the child being lifted up and comforted by its mother. Throughout life we continue to seek the comfort of those experiences which "uplift" us in an inspiring text, or the majesty of nature, or the power of art and music (Strozier 1997: 168). Religion, of course, with its promulgation of an ideal, divine reality as well as its use of sermons, readings, music, art, and liturgy, is a major source of that essential experience of feeling "lifted up" or inspired that is (for Kohut) at the core of idealization.

In footnotes to his seminal volume *The Analysis of the Self* (1971), Kohut suggests that the believer's experience of God "corresponds to the ancient omnipotent self-object, the idealized parent imago" (1971: 106). Earlier he wrote, in another footnote, that "the relationship to an idealized parent imago may have its parallel in the relationship (including mystical mergers) of the true believer and his God" (1971: 27). The experience of God may serve, then, as the carrier of that early idealization that was, and continues to be, necessary for a cohesive sense of self.

Mature narcissism and idealization, however, are very different from infantile narcissism. Development has taken place. Relatively free of object hunger, the mature self can choose the source of its narcissistic supplies. Rather than being emotionally driven and compulsively dependent, mature selfobject relationships are characterized by freedom, spontaneity, and realism. The mature self is able "to identify and seek out appropriate selfobjects – both mirroring and idealizable – as they present themselves in his realistic surroundings and to be sustained by them" (Kohut, 1984: 77). Maturity "does not make the self independent of selfobjects. Instead, it increases the self's ability to use selfobjects for its own sustenance, including an increased freedom in choosing selfobjects" (Kohut, 1984: 77). For Kohut this capacity to find empathic and responsive selfobject relations characterizes maturity and defines a successful psychoanalytic cure (Ornstein, 1998).

Thus Kohut's theorizing contains two implicit criteria for maturity, whether in personal relations, vocational choices, or concluding a successful analysis. First, the creation of continuing psychological structures so that the individual is not always lapsing into a state of object hunger and addictive dependency but is rather able to pursue a self-directed, nuclear program of goals and ambitions. Second, the ability to place oneself in affirming, responsive, and empathic relationships with others. I will argue momentarily that these two criteria are also very salient for the psychological analysis of the health or pathology of religious beliefs and practices.

It is important to note that Kohut's theorizing has two aspects that work together: a developmental theory and a functional analysis. Functions change throughout the developmental cycle. In earliest childhood, selfobjects function as a substitute for psychic structure not yet developed. If trauma occurs at this early stage, psychic structure never develops and so the person (even as a chronological adult) remains totally and desperately dependent upon external sources to perform these selfobject functions such as providing ideals to identify with or reinforcing a sense of self-esteem. This object hunger leads to narcissistic rage when these sources fail the narcissistically vulnerable adult. On the other hand, if there are gradual, phase-appropriate disappointments, transmuting internalization takes place. If that happens selfobjects can begin to function during later childhood as objects of internalization or agents of psychological structure-building as the child begins to develop some self-cohesion and to take over for herself the functions these external selfobjects once performed. Finally, if such self-structures develop, selfobjects function in adulthood to sustain the psychic structures now in place. The mature adult is still dependent on selfobjects but dependent in a very different way from the young child (or the narcissistic/borderline adult) who required (or requires) them to function in lieu of any internal self-structure.

For the mature adult, positive selfobjects do not just evoke soothing, or mirroring, or idealizing experiences, however emotionally powerful. They also facilitate the development of self-structure where it is lacking and nourish the self-structure that is in place. A powerful experience of romantic love or religious ecstasy may facilitate this developmental process if sufficient self-structure is in place; as Kohut says, oxygen in the air is not enough, you also need the physiological apparatus to make use of it. Or, if sufficient self-structure is not in place, such romantic and religious ecstasies may simply re-evoke early affective experiences. When they pass, such experiences leave the person just as object-hungry and dependent as ever. This is, presumably, what happens in the case of addictions where the substance continues to evoke a powerful affective experience but no new structure is laid down (Lichtenberg, 1991). There was a song popular in the USA a few years ago entitled "Addicted to love" which captures a certain kind of romantic desperation born of object-hunger. And perhaps the drive in many contemporary spiritual seekers who seem to only be seeking intense religious-like experiences through drugs, psychophysical manipulations, or intense ritual activities constitutes a kind of "addiction to mysticism."

This developmental perspective takes us beyond a rather facile self-psychology of religion which simply describes the selfobject functions of religious beliefs and practices (for example, Julian, 1992; Hedayat-Diba, 1997). Self-psychological analysis involves more than describing selfobject functions. It also involves uncovering potential and actual developmental pathologies in religious belief and practice (a similar point was made in reference to Hedayat-Diba by Woo and Mannes, 1997). Religious beliefs and practices certainly fulfill selfobject functions. But that does not, in itself, make them psychologically healthy on Kohut's definition, for addictive drugs and cult leaders also fulfill selfobject functions. To be healthful they must contribute to building psychological structures, support the self in its own nuclear program, and facilitate the self's location in an empathic, selfobject milieu. If, instead, religious beliefs and practices recapitulate a state of object hunger, or reinforce an addictive dependence, or denigrate the self in its search for its own unique goals and ambitions, then religion is in as much need of criticism by those who follow in the footsteps of Kohut as by those who follow in the footsteps of Freud. In Chapter 4 we will look more deeply at these problematic aspects of religion from a relational and self-psychological perspective.

LATER SELF-PSYCHOLOGICAL THEORIES

Self-psychology, the school of psychoanalysis that builds on Kohut's work, has undergone its own development in the years since Kohut wrote *The Analysis of the Self* and the essays in *How Does Analysis Cure?* Kohut's early writings show a clear debt to Heinz Hartmann and the school he helped found called ego-psychology. Freud had proposed that the ego – the seat of rationality within the personality – arose primarily in order to mediate between the biologically given and basically antisocial instincts of sex and aggression and the constraints imposed by society. Ego-psychologists like Hartmann and Erik Erikson argued not only that the ego was the result of conflict between individual drive and social constraint but that it had certain personal requirements of its own. The mature ego needed a solid identity, goals for the future, the mastery of skills, a sense of purpose, and values to guide action

(Hartmann, 1958). Hartmann and Erikson were quite explicit that religion could play a positive function in an individual's life by supplying the necessary values and providing moral guidance to the developing ego (Hartman, 1960).

Kohut's early emphasis on how selfobjects function to support and maintain the self is, in many ways, very analogous to Hartmann's theories about how, for example, ideals are necessary to support the ego. Writing in the 1970s, for example, Kohut sees a positive function for religion in supporting the self's activities in language very similar to that of ego-psychology:

> The recognition that the self arises in a matrix of empathy, and that it strives to live within a modicum of empathic responses in order to maintain itself, explains certain needs of man and illuminates the function of certain aspects of institutionalized religion, thus allowing us to appreciate certain dimensions of the culture-supportive aspects of religion and making it less necessary for us to see religion only as an illusion.
>
> (Kohut, 1978b: 752)

Apparently, in his own thinking about religion, Kohut continued in the approach laid out in his early, ego-psychological training and remained wedded primarily to this functional analysis of religious material rather than analyzing religion's developmental possibilities and pitfalls (Strozier, 1997: 166–72; Randall, 1984; Kohut, 1985: 261). Most of the recent applications of self-psychology to religion have continued in this rather limited approach of confining themselves to the analysis of the selfobject functions of religious practices.

In a seminal essay written in 1991 Lichtenberg charts self-psychology's development away from Kohut's primarily ego-psychological focus on selfobject functions towards redefining the term selfobject to refer, not to an object, but to a certain kind of experience, "an experience of cohesion and vitality of the self" (Lichtenberg, 1991: 470). Such a revision sweeps away Kohut's theorizing about the idealizing, mirroring, and alter-ego transferences which Lichtenberg sees as relics of Kohut's original reliance on ego-psychology (Lichtenberg, 1991: 460) and simplifies the term "selfobject" down to its clinically most important aspect – the experience of a vital sense of self. Lost in this process of theoretical simplification, however, is the detailed tracing of the vicissitudes of idealization (also mirroring and twinship) which can be very helpful in the analysis of cultural phenomena like religion and literature. While recognizing the clinical utility and experience-near power of this later, simpler formulation, in this essay I prefer Kohut's earlier, if more elaborate, theorizing about the developmental course of idealization because I think it illuminates one of the elemental dynamics of the religious life – idealization – and lays bare some of its developmental pitfalls.

The functional approach to the psychology of religion of Hartmann and Kohut contains the potential for a critical as well as descriptive approach to religion through the articulation of criteria with which to differentiate adaptive and non-adaptive forms of religion. Adaptive forms of religion support the self (ego) in its development and provide the wisdom and guidance necessary to traverse creatively the life-cycle. In addition, I am suggesting that Kohut's developmental theory contains the possibility of a wide-ranging critical approach to religion by calling attention to religion's role in manipulating the narcissistic needs and object hungers of its devotees as well as its provision of sustaining selfobject experiences. An account of both aspects of religion are necessary to a full psychology of religion.

There is one place where Kohut himself ventures beyond the purely functional approach to religion. In his essay on the "Forms and Transformations of Narcissism" (1978a) he breaks off his discussion of empathy and raises the topic of accepting death. His own death was almost twenty years in the future when he first presented this paper in 1965. If narcissism is the driving force in human personality, how is it possible for a person to accept the fact of her death? For Kohut such a radical acceptance cannot be authentic if it represents only a suppression of narcissism. To be authentic it must arise out of a transformation of narcissism. Such a transformation lies in the direction of what he calls "cosmic narcissism" that is "a shift of narcissistic cathexes from the self to a concept of participation in a supraindividual and timeless existence" (1978a: 456). Here individuals move from a life centered on the maintenance of the individual self, which is the self on which self-psychology focuses, to a life centering on a supraordinate Self, and their narcissism expands to embrace the cosmos at large.

Enlarging one's narcissism and identifying with a "supraordinate Self" enables one to achieve "the outlook on life which the Romans called living *sub specie aeternitatis* [from the perspective of eternity]" which is characterized not by "resignation and hopelessness but a quiet pride" (1978a: 455). The latter comment may be an aside at Freud, whose outlook was often characterized by resignation and hopelessness. For example, in reference to death Freud writes in *The Future of an Illusion*, "As for the great necessities of Fate, against which there is no help, they [humankind] will learn to endure them with resignation" (1964: 82). He insists that the only alternatives in the face of death are either religious illusions or Stoic resignation to the twin gods of "reason and fate" (1964: 88). Kohut is suggesting a third alternative – seeing life from the perspective of eternity. About this he writes, "I have little doubt that those who are able to achieve this ultimate attitude towards life do so on the strength of a new, expanded, transformed narcissism: a cosmic narcissism which has transcended the bounds of the individual" (1978a: 455).

Kohut relates this capacity for "cosmic narcissism" to the infant's identification with his mother. In that earliest stage too the individual ego is submerged in a relationship with the other. Kohut follows Freud in saying that memories of this earliest stage occasionally break forth into consciousness in the form of the "oceanic feeling" in which the individual feels merged with the universe or some transcendent reality. The scholar of Hindu philosophy Romain Rolland, after reading *The Future of an Illusion*, had written to Freud and suggested that such an "oceanic feeling" was the true core of religion, rather than the Oedipal belief in a divine father that Freud saw as the heart of religion. But Kohut contrasts his concept of cosmic narcissism with Rolland's idea of an oceanic feeling. "In contrast to the oceanic feeling, however, which is experienced passively (and usually fleetingly), the genuine shift of cathexes toward a cosmic narcissism is the enduring, creative result of the steadfast activities of an autonomous ego, and only very few are able to attain it" (1978a: 456). Cosmic narcissism is not a transitory "peak experience" but is rather an abiding attitude towards life and a deeper insight into the nature of reality. As a psychological definition of religion, such an expansion of empathy to include the cosmos is an alternative to both the oceanic mysticism of Rolland in which the self disappears into the Absolute and the legalistic monotheism of Freud in which the self must continually struggle to conform itself to a set of prohibitions.

While developing from the state of infantile symbiosis, cosmic narcissism, unlike the "oceanic feeling," is not a regression to the fusion of infancy in which individuality and intentionality vanish.

Rather it is the result of disciplined activity, for "a genuine decathexis of the self can only be achieved slowly by an intact, well-functioning ego; and it is accomplished by sadness as the cathexis is transferred from the cherished self to the supraindividual ideals and to the world with which one identifies" (1978a: 458). In these brief and suggestive remarks, it would seem that Kohut is referring to some kind of psycho-spiritual practice in which "the span of the ego here is not narrowed; the ego remains active and deliberate," resulting in "a rearrangement and transformation of the narcissistic libido" (1978a: 457).

Kohut is clear that intellectual activity and discursive reason alone cannot bring about this transformation and transcendence of individual egoism, for "I believe that this rare feat rests, not simply on a victory of autonomous reason and supreme objectivity over the claims of narcissism, but on the creation of a higher form of narcissism" (1978: 454). Whereas psychoanalysis is often associated with an unswerving faith in autonomous reason alone, Kohut here implies that other forms of knowing and being are also required. (In a later chapter we will find Hans Loewald making exactly the same point.) While never elaborating further on this idea of cosmic narcissism, in an essay "On Leadership", he writes in reference to the late secretary-general of the United Nations, Dag Hammarskjøld, whose posthumously published diary revealed a mystical orientation,

> The survival of Western man, and perhaps of mankind altogether, will in all likelihood be neither safeguarded by "the voice of the intellect" alone, that great utopian hope of the Enlightenment and Rationalism of the 18th and 19th centuries; nor will it be secured through the influence of the teachings of the orthodox religions. Will a new religion arise which is capable of fortifying man's love for its old and new ideals . . . the transformation of narcissism into the spirit of religiosity . . . could it be that a new, rational religion might arise, an as yet uncreated system of mystical rationality. . .?
>
> (1985: 70)

Again, Kohut does not elaborate on the meaning of his calling for the "amalgamation [of psychoanalysis] with mystical modes of thinking" (1985: 71). In these brief remarks, however, he is clearly doing two things. First, he is pointing towards a new goal for psychoanalysis to supplement Freud's dictum of reason controlling instinct by calling for a more universal or cosmic love, "a higher form of narcissism" (1985: 72). Second, he is underscoring that such a cosmic narcissism will not come through ego rationality alone but will require something analogous to a spiritual practice built upon "a constructive mysticism" (1985: 71). Since neither intellectual argument nor assertions of will-power alone are sufficient, Kohut is clear that religion can be a major (perhaps the primary) force in this transformation of individual narcissism into a universal embrace.

Kohut's articulation of this ideal of cosmic narcissism parallels the developmental theories of Lawrence Kohlberg and James Fowler. Kohlberg proposes six stages in the development of moral reasoning. In the first two stages, which he calls "pre-conventional," right and wrong are simply a function of direct, often physical consequences to oneself. Right and wrong are what you get rewarded or punished for. There is no larger moral framework beyond the immediate consequences of an act. The next two stages Kolhlberg labels as "conventional." Here right and wrong involve conformity to the conventions and mores of one's group or society. The final two stages are "post-conventional" in that the individual can now stand back and evaluate the standards of her culture and choose which to accept and which to reject. Now, for example, civil disobedience in the name of a higher set of principles becomes a rational possibility.

After elaborating these six stages in the development of moral reasoning, Kohlberg felt it necessary to speculate on the need for a seventh stage that he called a "cosmic perspective." This seventh stage points to a moral framework that extends beyond the claims of individuals and societies. Earlier stages of moral development are regarded as "humanistic" while "stage seven" is cosmic and transcendental and serves to provide a more encompassing framework in which the moral life can be grounded. Such a moral vision embraces the universe as a whole and perhaps even a reality beyond the known universe (Kohlberg, 1981).

In a similar way, Fowler's stages of what he calls "faith development" progress from the most immediate to the most universal. The early stages involve very concrete and literalistic approaches in which religious language is simply assimilated to the immediate world of the young child. God is a huge person who lives high in the sky. In adolescence religion supports the teenager's sense of belonging to a group, paralleling Kohlberg's "conventional stages." Later the young adult may develop the cognitive capacity to analyze such beliefs and choose to accept, reject, or reinterpret them. The final stage involves a universal attitude in which there is a "transnarcissistic love of being" and a lived experience of "unity with the one beyond the many" (Fowler, 1987).

Like Kohut, Kohlberg and Fowler regard such universal ethical and religious attitudes as a rare achievement but one that should serve as an exemplar for humanity. For them, this universalizing sensibility lies beyond the limits of normal psychological development. Such a transcendental outlook requires the capacity to stand back and look at one's life from a distance, to develop a realistic perspective on one's self, to come to terms with the transitoriness and finitude of individual life, and a "making peace with the cosmos" (Kohlberg, 1891).

Kohut, Kohlberg, and Fowler all agree that a religious practice is often an important ingredient in the transformation of egoism and individual narcissism into this cosmic love and universal attitude. Religious teachings often focus on the transitoriness of human existence and call to mind our connection to a greater reality (for example, the Tao, the divine existence, the cosmic law) that dwarfs and encompasses our individual concerns. Religious disciplines like meditation, communal worship, and devotional activities can evoke an experience of connection to a greater and more encompassing reality, that "supraordinate Self" that constrains and limits our individual selfishness. Thus religion can serve to reduce the egoism that interferes with a more cosmic sensibility. This, then, is part of the ambiguity of religion – a theme we will be addressing throughout this book: how can the same traditions give rise to the highest and most exemplary stages of human evolution and also sponsor some of the worst atrocities in human history?

THE NARCISSISM OF EVERYDAY LIFE

A friend of mine used to say that Kohut did for narcissism what Freud did for sex: remove the shame attached to it and reframe it as a normal part of human life. Kohut's writings imply that, whereas in Freud's day guilt surrounded sexual desires and so a network of defenses were constructed around them, in the present day shame surrounds narcissistic needs and so they become surrounded with defenses which, along with weaknesses in the self-structure, distort and constrict the personality. We all need an empathic selfobject milieu if we are going to experience optimal self-cohesion and vitality. We need places where we can feel ourselves a part of something greater than our individual egos, where our thoughts and feelings are received empathically, where our authentic goals and ambitions are supported by others. This is not just a refuge or retreat from the harshness of the quotidian world, it is an ongoing requirement for there to be joy, creativity and resiliency in our lives.

But our selfobject needs can be sabotaged either from within or from without. Those driven by object hunger cannot make use of the support available to them in the environment. They rage at any perceived failure of empathy. They drain dry the emotional resources of those around them. They seek to make themselves central in every interaction. Others lacking in self-structure may too quickly give up on themselves and resign themselves to situations that lack empathy, that denigrate their own desires, that undermine their own goals and ambitions. They may feel shame at their own need for emotional support. They may find it impossible either to identify their own goals and desires or to mobilize themselves to achieve them. They may remain stuck and dependent in relationships, jobs, or social and religious groups that play upon their lack of self-esteem and self-efficacy and undermine their autonomy and sabotage their initiative.

Thus, narcissistic needs must be met but narcissistic pathologies must be transformed through a reactivated process of self-structural development. This requires an empathic and supportive context in which the needs for idealization, mirroring, and twinship, which have been unmet since childhood, can begin to be fulfilled, in which the destructive patterns that sabotage their satisfaction can be confronted directly, in which new transmuting internalizations can take place. Often this means psychotherapy, although it is possible for an exceptionally gracious friendship or community to facilitate this process.

While the primary source of selfobject experiences comes from other people, the beauty of nature, the inspiration of poetry and music, the lure of ideals like truth and justice, all contribute to self-cohesion. The capacity to be moved by art, uplifted by music, awe-struck by nature, inspired by a text, or motivated by an ideal are as much signs of healthy selfhood as comforting a friend, being empathic with a lover, or supporting a child in her choices. All of these healthy selfobject processes have found a place within lived religion.

Chapter 2

Clinical illustrations

STANLEY: THE FAILURE OF IDEALIZATION AND OBJECT HUNGER

If the need for idealization is not met, if a child is not allowed to idealize, or if idealized objects fail too early, the child may block the capacity to idealize. Such a person cannot idealize, cannot commit themselves to any ideals, cannot fall madly in love, must disparage and debunk everything. But the need for objects of idealization does not disappear. It may become unconscious; from there it propels the individual into a frantic search for objects of idealization that are sooner or later bound to fail and so further reinforce his/her cynical attitudes. Such cynicism may also serve as a defense against the desperate hunger for an object of idealization.

Stanley was a very successful musician when he came to see me. He was rather obsessive and perfectionistic in his temperament but that served him well in his career as a cellist. He practiced several hours a day and was never satisfied with any of his performances. He played first cello with his local symphony orchestra, belonged to a chamber ensemble with whom he had made several recordings, and taught at a local music college where he also gave individual lessons.

Stanley's mother came from a family of concentration camp survivors. Given to paralyzing panic attacks, she was continually in a state of anxiety about her children getting sick, having accidents, or being kidnapped. She could not sleep at night while her children were on dates or with friends, and she made them feel so guilty about the anxiety they caused her that Stanley and his younger sister rarely went out during high school. Stanley described his mother as "being afraid of her own shadow."

Stanley's father was a high school teacher. He was beloved by only the best of his students; average students had no use for him or he for them. He was merciless in the grading of papers, often concluding with sarcastic comments to the students about "maybe you should try the vo-tech" or "this paper reads like it was written by someone with a room temperature IQ." He treated Stanley like one of his students. He insisted on reading all his son's homework assignments and correcting them, disparaging Stanley's work, and, if he really didn't like it, tearing the paper to shreds before Stanley's face and insisting another be written. Whenever Stanley tried to complain to his father, he was told that these things were being said and done out of love, that they were not meant personally or meanly but rather to facilitate Stanley's learning.

In music Stanley found something in which he could excel, and since his father had no interest in music, he was in no position to criticize his son's performances. In the compositions of Bach and Mozart Stanley found perfection, even if his renderings of them could never reach that exalted level. Music was the only domain that never disappointed him, although he was continually disappointed in himself, in his performance of it.

In his twenties he had gone on a series of religious quests. In college he became fascinated with Tibetan Buddhism and after graduating moved to a Tibetan Buddhist center in a western state of America. For two years he immersed himself in the routine of a semi-monastic life. Arising in the middle of the night to meditate and chant. Eating a light breakfast. Spending the morning practicing the cello and the afternoon in classes in Tibetan language and tradition. He describes this as one of the happiest times of his life. But this blissful world collapsed when he discovered that the leader was carrying on affairs with several of the women initiates and was also battling alcoholism.

Stanley says at that moment something just turned over inside himself. He felt sick. He barged into the center's office and called the leader a hypocrite and a charlatan. The man whom he'd told friends was an enlightened master he now threatened with a lawsuit. He packed his few belongings and took his cello and left the center without a second thought.

Depressed and depleted, music was his only comfort. He moved in with a friend from college with whom he'd kept in touch. His friend was a high school music teacher in a medium-sized Midwestern city and was able to get Stanley a job with the local symphony orchestra. One of the violinists was a young woman named Beth, who took an interest in Stanley, inviting him over for dinner (she lived with her parents) and to the movies. He described her as very plain-looking but sweet. She was also a Pentecostal Christian and Stanley began accompanying her to her charismatic meetings. He was quickly swept up in the emotional fervor. He cried as he heard stories of members of the group visiting each other in the hospital, taking care of each other's children, and even rebuilding a member's house damaged in a fire. He felt energized and elated, states attributed to the working of the Holy Spirit. He reports that his playing at this time had a power never again duplicated.

However, after six months of belonging to the fellowship, the pastor preached one night against evolution and Darwinism. Stanley was aghast at this level of anti-intellectualism. On the way home in the car he discovered that Beth did not believe in evolution either. They had their first real argument then. He called the preacher an imbecile and an ignoramus. People whom he had lavishly praised the week before for their warmth and mutual concern, he now called a herd of mindless sheep. That night Stanley could not sleep. The next morning he resigned his seat in the orchestra and left town.

Fortuitously the month before he had received a letter from the music director of an early music society in the New York area who had been in town and heard Stanley's playing in the local symphony orchestra. The letter offered him a position in New York. The other members of the chamber orchestra welcomed him, and helped him find a room in a rooming house and learn his way around New York. Within a year the group had made its first recording and Stanley had been offered a job at a small music school.

Stanley's ex-wife was a former student at that school. She never aspired to be a serious musician. She came from a rather wealthy family and attended the music school out of interest rather than to prepare for a career. She had initiated the relationship with Stanley, showing up at his office, expressing an interest in coming to hear him perform. They began dating immediately and were married within six months. Given her background, she tried to introduce Stanley to some of the finer, or at least more expensive, things of life. But he found himself disparaging them. For example, on his birthday she took him to a very expensive New York restaurant but all he could do was make snide remarks about the food. The soup was way overpriced; the idea of different wines for different courses was just a way of padding the bill; chocolate mousse was just chocolate pudding with a pretentious title. A year later they divorced; her parting words to him were "You could rain on anybody's parade."

In our first meeting Stanley spent most of the hour attacking psychotherapy. He knew he was depressed and his playing was suffering but he felt it must be biochemical and that drugs were the answer, except he was afraid they would dull his creativity. He was sure psychotherapy was just a con game that would be of no help to him. He no longer had any interest in religion since he knew from first-hand experience that it was all either hypocrisy or superstition or both. There was a Catholic church down the street from his apartment and he would often begin a session by sneering at the people he saw going to Mass. Nor had he found another relationship after his divorce two years earlier. The dating scene was described as a "meat market." He briefly joined a group for singles interested in classical music but dismissed them all as "a bunch of dilettantes." He went out once with a woman who described herself as a writer, but when he found out that she mostly freelanced stories for women's magazines he started referring to her as a comic book author.

The purpose of this case is not to describe a long and tortuous course of treatment. Rather it illustrates two routes that the failure of idealization can take that are relevant to understanding the psychology of religion. The failure of idealization can lead to an emotionally driven search for objects that are, at the beginning, idealized uncritically and, later, denigrated completely. It can also result in the inability to make commitments, to share in ideals, and in the cynical drive to disparage the commitments and ideals of others. Religion is a fertile ground for both of these dynamics. Its devotees often display a compulsive and untempered exaltation of their objects of devotion. Its critics often display an unrelenting drive to rid the world of any vestiges of idealization and illusion. These may well be two sides of the same coin. The rejection of idealization in love or religion may conceal a deep-seated conflict between the strong desire for idealization and a need to disparage it.

MARGE: IDEALIZATION AND DEPRESSION

Marge turned thirty the year she came to see me. A successful scientist with a software company, she complained of recurrent depression. A week before calling me she had found herself staring at a kitchen knife, debating about suicide. Horrified at how close she had come to injuring herself, and realizing the grip that such impulses had over her, she sought treatment.

She had recently moved to the New York area from California to take a job in a high-tech company. Graduating from Stanford with a degree in mathematics, she had always planned on going on to graduate school in that field. Upon learning of the high salaries computer firms were paying, however, she immediately went to work at one. She lasted there less than a year, quitting for reasons that seemed vague and unclear as she first described them. She had no trouble finding another job at more money, worked there two years, and then quit because she said she didn't get a promotion she felt she deserved. Immediately she got another job in the computer industry, this time at a very small and much more theoretically oriented company.

She described this as her happiest job, but after a year this company was bought by a major national software company in order to take over one of her company's applications. The new owners kept two of the men who worked on this one application and let everyone else go with a very generous severance package. So generous that Marge didn't have to work at all for two years. So she didn't. Instead she rented a cabin in a remote area of California and spent her time reading novels, self-help books, and texts on higher mathematics and keeping in touch with other mathematicians on the Internet.

Marge grew up in a suburb of Chicago in a family she described as "depressingly ordinary." Her father had migrated to the United States in his twenties, worked his way through college, where he trained as an electrical engineer, and in his forties established his own consulting firm. Marge describes him as totally work-oriented, success his single motivation. He did not work for the money – driving used cars and never owning a business suit – but, she thought, to prove something about himself. Her mother never went to college or worked outside the home. The oldest of two children, Marge reported always feeling closer to her father, even though she rarely saw him while growing up. She recalled that as soon as her younger brother was born, all her mother's attention went to him. Marge claimed she never missed it all that much as she had little respect for her mother. Growing up she felt more intelligent than her mother or brother. Her brother was described as "bright enough" but more interested in his friends and the latest fads in gadgets and clothes.

Good in maths and science, Marge found she could get close to her father by sharing his engineering interests and outlook on life, but this made her feel simply like an extension of her father's drive for success. Looking back she said that he was trying to propagate his dreams through her life. On one hand she felt controlled by these expectations. On the other hand, they oriented her in the world and gave her a sense of direction and a guarantee of her father's acceptance and that of the wider society.

As we examined her first two work experiences, a common pattern emerged. She went into them overflowing with enthusiasm for the work and the company. The projects were the most interesting, co-workers were all geniuses, company prospects the rosiest in the industry. But after a while the projects started to feel pedestrian and beneath her; co-workers weren't so sharp; managers were inept. She would lose interest and not come to work or find herself constantly arguing with everyone around her. In both cases, it turned out she had quit in a huff.

Her studies in maths and science, and later the jobs she was hired to do, involved more for her than just the mastery of the subject and a chance to do meaningful and interesting work. They also carried a hunger for the acceptance and approval, for the idealizing and twinship experiences that she did not receive from a distant father and an uninvolved mother. Out of those needs she constructed a very idealized approach to job and school. When they didn't fulfill these deep-seated narcissistic needs, the result was a big crash, a disappointment that became a serious depression.

A job had to be idealized, had to be perfect, in order for her to invest herself in it. If it didn't promise to fulfill her ideals, she had no energy for it. This very idealized, perfectionistic view of her career, which was necessary in order for her to mobilize herself to work for it, inevitably led to a disappointment. Thus she felt her life had been a history of disappointments. And so it was, since no job could supply her with the ideal environment in which everyone fully appreciated her and saw things exactly as she did.

While not involving religion, Marge's story illustrates another aspect of the dynamics of idealization. A hunger for objects of idealization can set a person up for depression and even suicide since any job, relationship, social institution, or religion is inevitably bound to fall short of overly idealized expectations. In Chapter 4 we will see several examples of religions that play upon the hunger for uncritical idealization and so captivate those who need something to be overly idealized before they can commit themselves to it. The cycle of emotionally driven and heightened expectations necessary to mobilize commitment, and leading to bitterness, cynicism, disappointment, and depression, can be seen in religious seekers as well as in occupational settings and intimate relationships. Often this cycle results from an early failure of idealization and the attempt to use a religion, a job, or an intimate relationship to substitute for what Kohut would call a missing self-structure, in this case the capacity to fully invest oneself emotionally in realistic (rather than overly idealized) projects, goals, and institutions.

Chapter 3

A psychology of the sacred

Now we can return to the question with which we began: What does it mean psychologically to call a teacher, an institution, an object, an experience, a text, or a ritual action "sacred" and to relate to it in that special way? One of the elements that goes into that attribution is the dynamic of idealization. To denote something as sacred is, among other things, to form what Kohut, in his earlier writings, would call an idealizing transference with it. We call something sacred when it meets our needs for idealization, when we can invest our narcissistic energy in it. That is why, as we have seen, idealizing language runs through much religious discourse.

ÉMILE DURKHEIM ON THE SACRED AND THE PROFANE

Many phenomenological definitions of the sacred stress its contrast with the profane. This begins with Émile Durkheim, writing at the end of the nineteenth century. Durkheim insists that the contrast between the sacred and the profane is a universal characteristic of religion (1965: 54). He does not argue for this claim but simply asserts it. He goes on to say that the sacred–profane distinction is not only a contrast but "that it frequently degenerates into a veritable antagonism. These two worlds are not only conceived of as separate, but as even hostile and jealous rivals of each other" (1965: 55). This opposition of sacred and profane forms Durkheim's first criterion for calling something a religion: "the real characteristic of religious phenomena is that they always suppose a bipartite division of the whole universe, known and knowable, into two classes which embrace all that exists but which radically exclude each other" (1965: 56).

Durkheim also notices that "systematic idealization is an essential characteristic of religions" (1965: 469) and he too insists that it is "a condition of [our] very existence" (1965: 471). But he rejects the idea that there is anything psychological about it. Rather, for Durkheim, "this reality . . . which is the universal and eternal objective cause of these sensations *sui generis* out of which religious experience is made, is society" (1965: 465). Starting from the observation that the behavior of crowds can be radically different from that of individuals, he argues that

> if collective life awakens religious thought on reaching a certain degree of intensity, it is because it brings about a state of effervescence which changes the conditions of psychic activity. Vital energies are over-extended, passions more active, sensations stronger; there are even some which are produced only at this moment. A man does not recognize himself; he feels himself transformed. In order to account for the very particular impressions he receives . . . above the real world where his profane life passes, he has placed another, which, in one sense, does not exist except in thought, but to which he attributes a higher sort of dignity than to the first . . . it is an ideal world.
>
> (1965: 469)

For Durkheim, then, religious idealizations arise when an individual is caught up in the collective effervescence of a crowd and transported into a state that transcends the consciousness of an individual. The individual then attributes such extraordinary experiences to an extraordinary and transcendental source, rather than to the functioning of group dynamics. Such experiences are powerfully transformative and do have their source in an idealized reality transcending the individual – that is, society – but not in any reality transcending the material world.

Durkheim's understanding of idealization, especially in the domain of religion, depends upon his theory of the relationship of the individual to society in which the self is totally subordinate to the social system. There is a certain reification of "culture" here. Social systems are superordinate realities that seem to exist above and beyond the world of lived experience. They create the dynamics of individuals' personalities by their supremacy over the individual. Selves appear wholly constituted by the internalization of the structures of culture. Such a framework enabled Durkheim to objectify society, making society the fundamental reality in human experience and an object of study. He thereby created a "scientific" sociology in which the observer stood apart from another culture and studied it objectively.

Durkheim assumed that the "primitive self," like that described in *The Elementary Forms of the Religious Life*, was completely encapsulated in its culture. Therefore Durkheim did not have to investigate the actual lived experience of individuals within these cultures for he assumed that their selfhood was totally constituted by their culture. Thus the structures of selfhood could be examined objectively, scientifically, by studying cultural forms and no heed need be paid to the actual, subjective (and therefore unscientific) experience of the people. It is not clear whether Durkheim would apply the same analysis to his own experience and those of his educated, European contemporaries and theorize his own experience and outlook as totally captive to his culture and devoid of subjectivity and intentionality.

Durkheim's implication that all dimensions of human life can be grasped by studying what is visible in the public sphere contains a vicious circularity. Such a conclusion – that he has exhaustively accounted for the nature of the religious life by describing religions' earliest public forms – represents the inevitable consequence of his assumption that all human experience is merely reflective of social structures. Thus he seems to have mistaken conclusion for methodological assumption.

There may be a difference between the meaning a ritual (for example) has for the culture and for the individual. A patient who belonged to a very conservative, patriarchal tradition once described for me how in her own mind she substituted the word "Goddess" and a mental image of a female form for the word "God" every time she heard it during her church's services. A contemporary Durkheimian might argue that this split between public and private consciousness characterizes modern, Western culture but not the cultures Durkheim studied. That may be true. My point is that that is an assumption and there is no way to check it if all that one investigates are public practices and beliefs. It is simply not clear that the sociological categorization of cultural activities is always the same as the lived experience and meaning of those activities for those who participate in them.[1]

CULTURE, SUBJECTIVITY, AND PSYCHOANALYSIS

This is currently a highly contested area in the social sciences. Many who refer to themselves as cultural constructivists take a position very similar to Durkheim's – that individual consciousness and intentionality are entirely a reflection of cultural institutions. Again, it is not clear to me whether such theorists see their own social constructivist theories as simply the reflection of their cultural situation, and if so, what conclusions they draw from that about the claims they make. Or, whether they feel they also arrived at these theories through the use of critical reflection and advocate them as an act of intentional choice. And whether they would like others to be convinced by the power of their arguments as well.

At a deeper level, a psychotherapeutic exploration of the structures of an individual's consciousness often reveals idiosyncratic patterns of fantasy and experience that are much more complex and (in some cases) bizarre than simply the reflection of culture, as with my conservative, evangelical Goddess-worshiping patient. Durkheim seems to assume a common, singular meaning. But it is not clear that people (in any culture) are so univocal or that the most salient meaning (salient for whom? the participants? the social observer?) of a religious practice is the conventional one. In Durkheim's account, the experiences of religious devotees are not simply expressed through, conditioned by, or embedded within social structures, their religious life is collapsed into their public performances. The only meaning possible is the publicly visible and socially sanctioned one. The Durkheimian position also obscures the human capacity to rework cultural meanings and to create culture. Human creativity – in fantasy and public action – is not reflected here.

1 This analysis of Durkheim's theories grew out of discussions with Laura Melling and her undergraduate honors paper at Rutgers University in the spring of 1999. Afterwards I came across Nancy Chodorow's *The Power of Feelings* which covers much the same terrain in relation to more contemporary thinkers and with much more depth and power.

In many ways Durkheim's model of the relationship of individual and society parallels that of Freud, who, in *Totem and Taboo*, also explores this relationship through a discussion of Totemism. Both Freud and Durkheim claim that Totemism represents the earliest form of religion. For Freud too, culture coercively imposes its structures (primarily restrictions on instinctual release) on the self. But Freud's model is more complicated than Durkheim's, since these very same structures are seen as arising out of the internal dynamics of the individual, particularly the Oedipal complex.

Totem and Taboo casts the Oedipal drama backward in time so that Freud's theory of the origin of the individual's conscience becomes the model for the origin of culture. For Freud ambivalence is the key to understanding the genesis of culture. Freud's narrative tells the story of how, after acting out their jealousy and hatred by killing the patriarch who had ruled over the primal horde of *Homo sapiens* and kept all the women to himself, the other side of the patriarchal sons' ambivalence emerged. Love replaced hate. At first the sons hated their father, who stood in the way of their boundless desire for power and sex. But they loved and admired him too. After murdering him, their affection for him, which they had to deny in order to kill him, reappeared as guilt and remorse. Thus guilt, on which all culture and religion depends, appeared. Freud writes, "We cannot get away from the assumption that man's sense of guilt springs from the Oedipus complex and was acquired at the killing of the father by the brothers banded together" (1962: 78–9).

Cultural institutions are, therefore, defenses against the drive toward incest and murder. A "memorable and criminal deed was the beginning of many things – of social organization, of moral restrictions, and of religion" (Freud, 1950: 142). The resolution of the Oedipal drama and the internalization of the power of the father becomes the core of culture: "religion, morals, society and art converge in the Oedipus complex . . . the problems of social psychology, too, prove soluble on the basis of one single concrete point – man's relation to his father" (1950: 157).

For Durkheim (and many contemporary cultural constructivists) there is a one-way causal arrow from social structure to individual consciousness. For Freud there is a dialectic whereby psychological dynamics (especially the Oedipal complex in males) create culture, and culture, through its prohibitions, in turn impacts the individual. (For more on Freud's approach to culture, see Jones, 1996.)

The implicit relation between the individual and culture is even more complex in relational psychoanalysis, especially British object relations theorists like Winnicott and Fairbairn. For Durkheim the self appears as the passive recipient of social forms, and for Freud there is an inevitable antagonism between selfhood and civilization. For Fairbairn the self is inherently relational. Both Freud and Durkheim see culture as a coercive force; it is primarily a modality of social control. For Fairbairn, on the other hand, culture does not have to be coercively imposed on the individual in the service of either instinctual control or the formation of selfhood, since, for Fairbairn, relationality is constitutive of selfhood. Freud begins with antisocial drives that he has to domesticate through the Oedipal struggle. The institutions that result from this can only be carriers of the Oedipal submission to the law of the father. Fairbairn begins his theorizing from pro-social, inherently relational human beings. Communal life is its natural expression.

For Winnicott, culture arises naturally out of true-self creativity. Winnicott begins his theorizing from what he calls "a third area of human living, one neither inside the individual nor outside in the world of shared reality" (1971:110). This "intermediate area of experience" starts with children playing. Play stands at the interface of the outer world and the world of inner psychological process.

> Into this play area the child gathers objects or phenomena from external reality and uses these in the service of some sample derived from inner or personal reality . . . In playing, the child manipulates external phenomena in the service of the dream and invests chosen external phenomena with dream meaning and feeling.
>
> (1971: 51)

At first, in her playing, the child uses toys and other objects that she invests with special meaning. This creative capacity, however, continues to develop after the toys have been put aside. Toys are the catalysts of the creative capacity. When they recede into the background, there remains the residue of the inventiveness that generates art and the curiosity that drives science, that is, the capacity to create culture. In a moving passage about the fate of these childhood "transitional objects," Winnicott writes,

> It is not forgotten and it is not mourned. It loses meaning, and this is because the transitional phenomena have become

> diffused, have become spread out over the whole intermediate territory between "inner psychic reality" and "the external world as perceived by two persons in common," that is to say, over the whole cultural field. At this point my subject widens out into that of play, and of artistic creativity and appreciation, and of religious feeling, and of dreaming.
>
> (1971: 5)

Creativity begins from the interpersonal matrix of infant and parent, develops through play and culminates in the symphonies of Beethoven, the paintings of Rembrandt, and the theories of Einstein. "For cultural experience, including its most sophisticated developments. . . . [is] in direct continuity with play, the play of those who have not yet heard of games" (1971: 100).

The creation of culture, for Winnicott, begins with children playing, thereby developing their capacities for spontaneous creativity. These capacities generate the art and music and science that are the staples of culture. Thus cultural forms are more an expression of human selfhood and vehicles for the self's creative expression than they are impositions upon it. For neither Fairbairn nor Winnicott does the life of society exist over and above the individual (as Durkheim implies). Rather the individual and the social world exist in a mutual, reciprocal relationship to each other. Culture is as much an expression of subjectivity as a determiner of it. They exist together in a system of mutual interaction. A relational psychoanalytic perspective on human nature preserves the importance of subjectivity and intentionality without sundering the individual from culture and it retains a place for imagination and creativity.[2]

The psychoanalyst who probably thought the most about the relationship of culture and the individual was Erich Fromm. Trained in philosophy and sociology before he studied clinical psychoanalysis and open to Marxist as well as Freudian theory, Fromm was an exceptionally multidimensional thinker. Fromm's notion of "social character" represents his attempt to theorize the interplay of culture and subjectivity. For Freud, patriarchal family structures were universal, rooted in biology. Repressive social structures and

2 The same point about Winnicott and culture is discussed in Flax, 1990. The relationship of selfhood and society in relational psychoanalysis is discussed in more depth in Jones, 1996.

the guilt they engender were natural and inevitable. For Fromm, familial relations represent the general patterns of a given society and are not universal. Societies organize families in order to provide the character styles that society needs to function. Society structures the family, and the family, in turn, structures the developing child so that most members of a society share a certain common core of character traits which Fromm calls their "social character" (Fromm, 1947).

Repression, then, is not only an intrapsychic process but also a social one. Society shapes and structures consciousness by allowing some elements of the personality to enter awareness and others to be repressed. Medieval society needed dutiful serfs and peasants, and its authoritarian family structure taught children to repress most of their initiative and autonomy and so prepared them to take their places as good citizens of the feudal church and society. Capitalism needs dutiful workers and desperate consumers and so makes social acceptability contingent on consumption. Thereby producing what Fromm calls the "marketing personality" who sees the self as a commodity to be packaged and exchanged for the approval of others. Along the way other values besides consumption – intellectual, artistic, spiritual ones – are repressed (Fromm, 1947).

This happens, Fromm says, because we are basically alone. Born into a symbiotic bond, development breaks that bond and gives us more and more autonomy but at the price of isolation and loneliness. We attempt to overcome that loneliness and isolation by giving away our autonomy and submitting unconsciously to the group norms out of a need to maintain a tie to others.

Just as repression has a social dimension, so too, for Fromm, does psychoanalysis and uncovering the unconscious. Making the unconscious conscious and rediscovering what Fromm calls "the true self" undoes the repression that society forces upon us. Uncovering the true self is an act of social, as well as personal, transformation. By becoming conscious of them, Fromm holds out the hope that we can, to some extent, transcend these pressures for conformity and live freely and creatively.

Fromm, who served as the head of the social psychology department at the Frankfurt Psychoanalytic Institute in the 1930s and practiced as a psychoanalyst and analytic supervisor till the end of his life, illustrates one possible combination of clinical psychoanalysis and social analysis. Fromm provides something missing from Durkheim's social constructionist model: an account of how social structures become psychological structures, how social forms become transformed into the character and style prominent in that society. For Fromm, as for Freud, the key to this process is repression. Society forms personality by the repression of those aspects of the self not valued by the culture.

Society, however, does not simply subsume individual subjectivity for Fromm. Increased awareness of the ways society shapes us creates the possibility of making choices about society's impact upon us and of constructing our own personal meanings out of the materials culture provides us. Fromm calls this capacity to become self-aware, to develop a critical perspective on our culture, and to make some choices in relation to culture, "transcendence." Fromm then seeks to do justice to both the role of culture in shaping consciousness and the reality of individual subjectivity or "transcendence." Thus Fromm too presents a more dialectical model of the interplay of culture and subjectivity.

A more contemporary relational theory might substitute the category of internalization for Fromm's category of repression as the mediator between culture and selfhood. For example, one of the major characteristics of contemporary culture appears to be our obsessive need for control. So often it seems we feel we need to control everything: our moods, the economy, the weather, the functioning of our bodies. In my clinical practice, that fear of losing control often appears as a major symptom of our era. Hypertension and other stress disorders, sexual dysfunction, and anxiety attacks frequently occur when contemporary men and women fear they are losing control over some part of their life.

This demand for control often insinuates itself into contemporary family life. As the cultural ethos of detachment and control shapes family life, child-rearing is increasingly influenced by these same values. Parents often bring their children to therapy not to improve communication or learn to understand them better but only to ensure that the kids will turn out as they expect them to, like products off an assembly line.

There appears a connection between the cultural privileging of the technological values of predictability, detachment, and control and the fear of emotion. Feelings seem outside the hegemony of rationality. They threaten to upset our carefully planned and controlled lives. Often their existence is simply denied. These values of efficiency, detachment, control, and the suppression of emotion, when they enter the family, run counter to children's needs for empathy, understanding, and being accepted for who they are as individuals. Children raised in such an ethos may learn to suppress their own emotions, to become more detached, and less able to enter spontaneously into intimate relationships.

This relational psychoanalytic perspective would agree with Fromm that society represents both certain cultural values, currently efficiency and control, and a certain personality style, currently often characterized by a brittle and defensive detachment. From a relational psychoanalytic standpoint, the emotional tenor of family relationships is the primary factor that is internalized and that makes up the foundation of the developing sense of self. And the emotional tenor of the family is, in turn, shaped by the values of the culture. I am suggesting that through this process of internalization the ethos of a culture is transformed into the structures of selfhood. Internalization, in which our early experiences are incorporated into our sense of self, rather than repression, is the bridge between culture and subjectivity. Such a perspective also preserves Fromm's insistence that individuals are not simply entombed in culture. Rather they possess the potential to construct personal meanings and critically evaluate cultural norms and, through increased awareness, make some choices about culture's impact.

Thus psychoanalytic theory, both Freudian and relational, portrays a much more nuanced and reciprocal relationship between self and society than Durkheim presupposes. Cultural institutions both arise out of human subjectivity and act back upon it. Psychoanalytic theories can be criticized for, in practice, not paying enough attention to their cultural context. In their theorizing, however, they not only recognize the impact of culture on consciousness: Freudian and relational theories complement this reality with an understanding of the human capacities to internalize and to create and recreate culture.

Since Durkheim's theory of religion rests upon a model in which the self is simply overwhelmed by overarching social forces, questioning the sufficiency of that model of the self casts doubt on the adequacy of his account of religion. If the individual interacts with culture rather than simply being subsumed by it, other sources, besides cultural effervescence, must be found for that core religious experience of feeling caught up in a greater reality.

For Durkheim, as long as people live in societies (and it is impossible for people not to) there will always be a religious dimension to human life: the experience of collective effervescence and the sense of being a part of something greater than the individual will always be there. Of course, Durkheim simply posits the capacity to be caught up in this collective state and to feel oneself connected to a greater (in his case, social) reality as well as the ability to internalize such experiences and to reflect upon them which, in his mind, gives rise to religious beliefs and doctrines. He does not inquire into any possible origin of such capacities within the lives of individuals. This is part and parcel of the problem we noted earlier: Durkheim simply ignores the subjectivity and agency of individuals within society; or, more precisely, he subsumes them into collective structures so that subjectivity and agency disappear into social relations.

Psychoanalytic theory will not let the matter rest there. Both Freud and Kohut, for example, theorize about the psychological origin of that capacity for being caught up in a greater, idealized reality that all these theorists take as the heart of religious experience. For Freud that experience begins with the child's, especially the boy's, relationship with the father who appears larger than life. Later this experience of protective dependency on the idealized father, if it is not renounced, is projected onto the surrogate father figure called God. Thus Freud writes, "I cannot think of any need in childhood as strong as the need for a father's protection... The origin of the religious attitude can be traced back in clear outlines as far as the feeling of infantile helplessness" (1962: 19).

Kohut's theory is less essentially gendered. The experience of "uplift," as we have seen, begins when the child (either boy or girl) is physically picked up and comforted by the parent (either father or mother). What is internalized from childhood as the psychological ground of religious experience is not the image of the parent (father) but rather the relational experience of being lifted up and comforted. Both Freud and Kohut offer an explanation for that capacity for uplift and idealization, which Durkheim simply presupposes, by grounding this experience in the subjectivity of individuals and the vicissitudes of their psychological history.

Nowhere does Durkheim attempt to derive the supposedly universal antagonism of the sacred and the profane from the fundamental collective experience that spawns religions, a point we will return to shortly. Rather the definition of the sacred as "that which the profane should not touch" (1965: 53) exists as a generalization from the totemic religions which Durkheim discusses in *The Elementary Forms of the Religious Life*. But no reason is given for the existence of such a dichotomy in human experience.

Durkheim's argument underscores the importance of certain kinds of group phenomena in human life, including the religious life. He points to an important connection, especially in the domain of religion, between idealization, the sense of being a part of a greater reality, and experience of transformation to which we will return in a later chapter. And he is certainly right that it is "at the school of the collective life that the individual has learned to idealize" (1965: 470) as far as the content of religious (as well as political, artistic, scientific, and philosophical) ideas and practices are concerned. These contents are clearly provided by social institutions. But his claim to completely derive all aspects of religion, including its idealizations, from the effervescence that occurs in groups gives no account of what role such social ecstasy plays in the actual lived experience of people or what draws the person back again and again to engage in such behavior. To account for such phenomena a more psychological theory is required.

RUDOLPH OTTO AND THE EXPERIENCE OF THE HOLY

A parallel, and more psychological, phenomenology of the sacred–profane dichotomy can be found in Rudolph Otto's discussion of the experience of the holy as *sui generis*, that is to say, absolutely unique, in *The Idea of the Holy* (1958). Otto asserts that the authentic experience of the holy is unique and incomparable with any other human experience. Since this experience is so unique, no categories drawn from ordinary psychological life can apply to it for it is "perfectly *sui generis* and irreducible . . . while it admits of being discussed, it cannot be strictly defined . . . [or] taught, it can only be evoked, awakened in the mind" (1958: 7). Otto is not simply saying that the *holy* itself is beyond our categories and cannot be defined, he is saying that the human *experience* of the holy is also indefinable. Thus the experience cannot be analysed, only recalled to mind. Only evocative and not analytic language is appropriate. (A critique of Otto's position can be found in Proudfoot, 1985.) Thus Otto is the forerunner of those who would argue that religious experience contains an essential feature that forever lies beyond psychological scrutiny and even beyond human psychology altogether. On such grounds the psychology of religion would be impossible, or at least limited to the study of a few superficial religious behaviors.

But Otto's argument is surely confused. Anything that we experience must take place in and through our psychological apparatus. In order to experience it, internalize it, remember it, and draw upon it, in other words in order to be an *experience* at all, an experience must be mediated through our cognitive and neurological structures, and make contact with the psychological schemas which we have built up in the course of our personal histories. In other words any experience we have, even an experience of something beyond our ordinary reality, is inevitably psychological in that it is mediated through the cognitive categories and takes place in the psychodynamic context which psychologists study. (A further discussion and critique of Otto can be found in Jones, 1991.) Thus a psychology of religion not only is possible but is an important dimension of our understanding of religious phenomena, for it can help illuminate the cognitive and psychological structures through which all experience is mediated and can uncover the relationship between the types of religious experience and practice a person finds compelling (or aversive) and their personal history and development.

Of course the theological question, implicit in Otto's treatise, of whether the ultimate source of such an experience is a transcendental Other lies beyond the domain of psychology. Such a question must be answered positively or negatively on other, more philosophical, grounds. The psychologist can only insist that all such experiences are mediated in various ways. To go beyond that and insist that a description of such psychological mediation provides a complete account of such experiences is to fall into the trap of reductionism which seems highly problematic on philosophical grounds. (My own critique of reductionism can be found in Jones, 1996.)

The epistemological issue implicit in a psychological analysis of Otto's work, however, goes beyond the issue of reductionism. Implicit in Otto's work is the assumption, with which I concur, that knowledge arises out of experience. We have no authentic knowledge of God (or anything else) apart from experience. Without some experience to ground them, all the claims we make are abstractions and reifications. Otto is right in his basic insistence that the knowledge of God arises from the experience of God. One cannot set knowledge against experience as, for example, Karl Barth does in his *Commentary on the Letter to the Romans*, where he argues that our knowledge of God comes from a revelation that exists outside of, and even in opposition to, our human psychological capacities for experience.

Any and all experience, from which any and all claims to knowledge derive, inevitably has a mediated, psychological dimension. The experience is shaped by the cognitive structures we bring to it and our personal, psychological history has inclined us to be attracted by some elements of our experience and to repress others. Thus psychoanalysis, which unpacks just those connections between personal history and the types of knowing and doing that fascinate or repel us, is inevitably an epistemological enterprise. And Otto's claims about the nature of the holy, precisely because they arise out of his experience, inevitably have a psychological aspect to them too. No claim we make, in any field, can finally be separated from the psychology of those who make it and those who are convinced by it. The reality that knowledge in any field arises out of experience, means that all knowing inevitably contains a psychodynamic element.[3]

In addition, Otto often presents "the holy" as though "the holy" was an object we could experience directly. However, the whole point of the book, *The Idea of the Holy*, is the "the holy" is not an object in the world of time and space that can be experienced directly. This may simply be a fundamental inconsistency in Otto's theory. It may also point to an important aspect of any discussion of the "the holy" or "the sacred." The sacred or the holy is not an object at all but a characteristic of certain objects or experiences. Special books, buildings, trees, people are experienced *as* holy or sacred. In Otto's case, I am not experiencing an object called "the holy" or "the numinous" (his terms). Rather I am having an experience that has a "numinous" or "holy" quality to it. It may be an experience of nature, or of a text, or even of my own states of consciousness. But again, "the holy" is not itself an object I experience, rather it is a special way of experiencing various objects or states of consciousness. (For a discussion of possible psychological roots of such a way of experiencing, see Jones, 1991.)

A certain dualism between the experience of the holy and all

3 For an interesting psychological analysis of the psychodynamic roots of Otto's ideas of the *mysterium tremendum* in terms of Otto's own personal history, see Capps, 1997.

other experience, which parallels Durkheim's dualism of the sacred and the profane, marks Otto's account of religion. While insisting on the discontinuity between the experience of the holy and all our other experiences, Otto still seeks to describe the experience. But he underscores its uniqueness by coining a new set of terms, describing it as the *mysterium tremendum*, and he takes great pains to distinguish these feelings from the more ordinary, human emotions of fear, dread, or excitement. While recognizing antecedents to the *mysterium tremendum* in our ancestors' dread in the face of the awesome power of nature or their fear of the unknown, Otto writes,

> Any one who is capable of more precise introspection must recognize the distinction between such "dread" and natural fear is not simply one of degree and intensity. . . It has therefore nothing to do with intensity, and no natural fear passes over into it merely by being intensified. I may be beyond all measure afraid and terrified without there being even a trace of the feeling of uncanniness.
>
> (1958: 15)

Thus Otto's elaboration of the *experience* of the sacred contains the same "bipartite" structure as Durkheim's discussion of the social forms of religion.

At the core of the *mysterium tremendum* is the experience of being overpowered. Otto delineates three components that contribute to the experience of *tremendum*: first, "awefulness" or "dreadfulness" that gives rise to the sense of the wrath of God which feels "arbitrary" and "daunting" (1958: 18–19); second, the "aweful majesty" which goes beyond any ordinary feeling of being overpowered to an experience of utter nothingness producing a sense of humility (1958: 20); and finally there is the sense of "urgency" which generates the sense of God's willfulness and forcefulness (1958: 23). All of this reflects Otto's drive to portray how the experience of the holy differs from ordinary experience not simply "by degree or intensity" but rather as something "overwhelmingly great" (1958: 15). Both Durkheim and Otto, then, ground the experience of the sacred in the feeling of being overwhelmed and overpowered: by society in Durkheim's account and by the encounter with the holy in Otto's.

SPLITTING THE SACRED AND PROFANE

Psychologically there may be some connection between this focus on being overwhelmed by the experience of the holy (either as collective effervescence or as *mysterium tremendum*) and the dichotomizing of sacred and profane. Fairbairn addresses a parallel issue with his discussion of what he calls "the moral defense against bad objects." The moral defense represents Fairbairn's approach to the dynamics of idealization. The child begins absolutely dependent on his parents. If they are experienced as unavailable or untrustworthy or unable to care for the child or otherwise "bad," the child's existence feels threatened. He must do anything he can to make the world feel safe, even going so far as blaming himself for the experience of badness in order that the external, parental world can appear good. Fairbairn writes, "the child would rather be bad himself than have bad objects . . . one of his motives in becoming bad is to make his objects good . . . he is rewarded by the sense of security which an environment of good objects confers" (1943: 66).

In order to maintain the experience of the parents as "good," the child splits the sense of badness off from the parents and takes it on himself. Thus the child maintains an idealized view of the parents at his own expense, experiencing himself as bad and seeing the parents, on whose goodness he depends, as good. The child sanitizes the image of the parents at the cost of his own self-esteem and self-worth, protecting his idealization of them by taking the pain and pathology of their relationship into himself, bearing "the burden of badness" (Fairbairn, 1943: 65). Thus a dichotomy is created in the child's, and later the adult's, experience between an all-good, idealized, external object and an entirely bad self. A split that parallels exactly the dichotomy between the sacred and the profane found in Durkheim's and Otto's definitions of religion. In the "moral defense," idealization of the other is maintained at a cost to oneself. Relating to parents, or any other powerful, ideal reality, automatically generates the self-experience of being bad.

In that psychological context, called by Fairbairn the "moral defense," encountering an overpowering and idealized social effervescence or *mysterium tremendum* leads inevitably to a splitting of experience into good and bad, sacred and profane, domains. For idealizing the other means inevitably denigrating oneself and everything connected to oneself. It is not coincidence that Fairbairn uses theological language in which to describe the moral defense and the splitting that results from it when he writes, "it is better to be a sinner in a world ruled by God than to live in a world ruled by the Devil" (1943: 67). And it makes sense that Durkheim and Otto would move directly from an account of a collective effervescence or "aweful experience" that overwhelms the individual to a dichotomy of sacred and profane as supposedly the key to religion. So common is this splitting in religious communities.

Melanie Klein introduces the additional factor of the role of aggression into this discussion of bifurcating the world into good and bad, sacred and profane, compartments. Klein claims that the child is born with innate aggressive and pleasure-seeking drives, a theory derived from Freud's speculations about the life and death instincts. The infant fears that her own innate aggressiveness will destroy her, and so she removes this aggressiveness from herself by projecting it onto her mother. But now, of course, the infant fears she will be destroyed from the outside by the mother who now embodies the aggression originating in the infant. Klein terms this situation the "paranoid position" as it is characterized by anxiety over being persecuted by the mother.

Of course the infant also receives positive, pleasurable experiences from the feeding, cuddling, and other interactions with his mother. These experiences evoke her pleasure-seeking drive and are carried by the sense of the mother as good, pleasurable, and nurturing. The infant's experience is thus split between an image of the bad mother who threatens to annihilate the child and the good mother who provides satisfaction and pleasure. The relative health of the child and her later development hinges on the presence of enough good-mother experiences to contain and modulate the persecutory anxiety created by the child's projection of her own aggressiveness onto her mother.

Still the infant must keep the good mother from being destroyed by the destructiveness present in the infant's inner and outer worlds. To protect the good-mother experience, the child separates his image of her mother into distinct good-mother and bad-mother compartments. And since both the good-mother and bad-mother images are directly tied to pleasurable and fearful experiential states within the infant, the infant's experience of herself also becomes split into good-self and bad-self compartments. The rigidity of this splitting, which is designed to protect the good-mother and the good-self experiences from the destructive forces within and without, is directly proportional to the amount of positive caring the child has received. If the infant has received sufficient nurturance and care, she has built up enough positive experiences to modulate her fear of her destructiveness. Then she is not so anxious about it and doesn't need so rigidly to split off the good mother and the good self in order to protect them. If she has few positive emotional resources to draw on in dealing with her own aggressiveness, the infant is much more anxious about the power of aggression and so needs more drastically to split off and protect the good mother.

An insufficient supply of good-object experiences results in this more rigid and pathological form of splitting. As part of this defensive move, the goodness of the good object becomes exaggerated in the child's imagination as a counterbalance to the increased power of the persecutory, destructive mother. Thus splitting and idealization are defenses against persecutory, destructive forces. If the idealized, all-good mother fails in some way, the defense breaks down and the persecutory experience breaks through and the individual turns that aggression either on herself, in self-flagellating rages, or against the disappointing object, who becomes the object of intense anger. The rigidity of this splitting depends on the amount of persecutory anxiety, which, in turn, depends on the quality of early object relations.

Klein here makes an important distinction between the good mother and the idealized mother images. The good-mother image is a natural part of normal development and represents the carrier of the child's pleasure-seeking drive and positive early experiences. The good-mother image is thus relatively connected to reality. The idealized mother image, on the other hand, is a defense associated with more severe forms of splitting when it is necessary to ward off extremes of persecutory anxiety.

In the course of normal development, if the degree of splitting is not too severe, the child moves from the "paranoid position" to what Klein calls the "depressive position." If the child's ego is not weakened by too profound a splitting, the child can grow to tolerate ambivalence and to recognize that her mother as well as herself contains both good and bad aspects. The child then comes to accept that she can hate and love the same object and learns to deal with his destructiveness not by splitting but by making reparations and by reaching out in reciprocal care to the parent and to others. The child begins to take responsibility for her own destructive fantasies rather than projecting them onto the external world. In the best of all possible outcomes, the child learns to tolerate ambiguity, and that relational ties are strong enough to contain aggression, that splitting is not necessary, and that love is stronger than hate. (This presentation of Kleinian theory is drawn from her volumes, *Guilt and Reparation, 1921–1945* , and *Envy and Gratitude, 1946–1963* .)

If the balance of negative and positive early experiences was weighted towards the negative and too severe an internal split developed, and if later experiences failed to redress that balance, the individual enters adolescence and early adulthood with the twin defenses of splitting and over-idealization still in place. Unable to tolerate ambiguity and still burdened with rage and persecutory anxiety, the individual needs to continue to split the world into opposing camps of good and evil, to unrealistically idealize some object and protect it from contamination by segregating it from forces of impurity, and to externalize the persecutory rage in campaigns against threatening others. And, if an idealized person or institution proves imperfect, he will turn that rage on the object of his disappointment. (A similar point about the sacred–profane distinction from a Kleinian perspective was made by Lutzky, 1991.)

While theorizing its etiology very differently, Fairbairn and Klein both call attention to an often-seen clinical constellation that involves both splitting and idealization. Such splitting divides the world into completely opposed black and white camps in which things are either all good or all bad. Clinically (for example, as portrayed in the two cases in the previous chapter) one of the symptoms of the character pathologies marked by splitting is that others (including often the therapist) are first put on a pedestal. Then later, at the first sign of any slight imperfection, the overly idealized one is cast down into the darkest hell. For Fairbairn and Klein, the solution to splitting and the moral defense lies in the capacity to tolerate ambiguity. A major part of the treatment of such patients is helping them develop the capacity to tolerate ambivalence and ambiguity – a capacity that I take as a crucial sign of mental health.

Why should this be a marker of mental health? Or, to put it the other way, why should splitting and over-idealization be seen as psychopathological? A common sign of a diagnosable emotional disorder is that a behavior pattern interferes with a person's "social and occupational functioning." People who divide the world so rigidly into good and bad and see another person, job, or institution as all bad after even the slightest disappointment often have a history of conflicted and failed relationships and occupations. The concomitant tendency to demonize others often leads them into serious trouble socially. Such a history of conflicted relationships is probably sufficient reason to consider such a character style pathological.

In addition, William James in *The Varieties of Religious Experience* distinguishes two types of temperament: what he calls the "once born" or "healthy minded" who are relentlessly optimistic and Pollyannish and feel that just by thinking positively, all their troubles will cease; and the "twice born" or "sick soul" who is often in inner turmoil and conflict and seems always aware of suffering and diminishment. James says he favors the "twice born" because their view of the world encompasses more of reality. Something analogous may also be part of the problem with those who split the world, overly idealizing the "good" and overly demonizing the "bad." Most people and institutions in the world are ambiguous, are a mixture of negative and positive characteristics and actions. To be able to recognize and tolerate the inevitable ambiguities of others is to be able to face more of reality and incorporate more of reality into one's vision of life.

So we might regard splitting and over-idealization as pathological not only because of the trouble they often lead to but also because they can blind one to reality. In the next chapter we will describe various forms of religion that seem to engage in splitting, over-idealization, and the demonization of others. Like a person who displays such traits, such religions often do a great deal of harm socially. Does that make them psychopathological? That is a question we must consider later.

Durkheim and Otto can give no reason for the dichotomizing of the sacred and the profane that lies at the heart of their definition of religion. The relational psychoanalytic theories of Fairbairn and Klein suggest that such splitting and the idealizations it serves to maintain derive from the child's early relationship with its parents. Thus such a dichotomy is not inevitably a part of the religious consciousness (as Durkheim and Otto imply) but is rather a function of a certain psychodynamic (perhaps pathological) constellation and a certain defensive structure. Thus an opposition between the sacred and the profane may not be essential to religion. Fairbairn and Klein imply that where this dichotomy does exist, it may be a symptom of splitting, of an inability to tolerate ambiguity, and of a tendency to see everything in polarized, black and white, terms.

From Durkheim and Otto through the present, this dualistic

conception of the sacred has been very influential in theories of religion. It may not be coincidence that such a dualistic way of understanding the sacred arose in the waning days of a Western theology that has, for most of its history, emphasized the transcendence of divine reality, portraying a God set over against the world and a spiritual domain over against the physical one. This dichotomous structure of Western religious thought was taken up even by secular thinkers like Durkheim, as well as by those more overtly theological like Otto, in their theorizing about the sacred.

For Fairbairn and Klein (like Freud) idealization is connected to a character pathology in which some objects are experienced as all good at the expense of others, often the self, being experienced as all bad. Another variation of this splitting occurs when a person identifies with an idealized tradition or group and then projects the sense of badness onto some outside person or group, thereby seeing some other group, race, or religion as evil. The experience of badness that the individual has taken into himself is so painful that often it must be discharged by being projected onto a despised group. Religious groups that encourage this splitting of the world into all-good and all-bad camps must often find others to demonize and carry this sense of badness. We shall see several examples of this when we discuss religious fanaticism in the next chapter. If Durkheim and Otto were correct in claiming that the essence of religion involved being overwhelmed by an idealized and overpowering reality, then religion would have to be understood psychoanalytically as essentially pathological. For the dichotomizing of sacred and profane and the idealizations that accompany it would inevitably appear as signs of splitting and the moral defense. However, such splitting is not invariably a part of religious consciousness. Rather it may result from the combination of feeling overpowered by some idealized experience or institution and a personality characterized by a severe form of splitting.

In addition, for Kohut idealization is a natural and potentially non-pathological aspect of human life. A view of the sacred and its concomitant idealizations fashioned in the context of the dynamics of splitting separates the experience of the sacred from the rest of human experience. A Kohutian perspective, however, points out that there are also continuities between the psychological processes involved in the denotation of something as sacred and other human phenomena, especially romantic love and the ecstasies evoked by aesthetic encounters. The sacred does not have to be defined by an opposition to other domains of experience. It can also be understood (contrary to Otto) as the intensification or refocusing of the normal idealizations of everyday life. A Kohutian understanding of idealization suggests that these dualistic definitions of sacredness should be complemented by theorizing which stresses the continuity between the psychological processes underlying religion and those common in other human domains as well as between objects denoted as sacred and other objects.

In much of the history of religions, it is ordinary objects – tables, clothes, trees, cups and plates, books, human beings, interpersonal encounters – which become denoted as sacred. It is not the specialness of the object or experience but the kind of relationship with the object or experience that leads to the attribution of sacrality. The sacred is not, necessarily, a unique and special object or domain split off from the rest of life but is rather the world of ordinary objects experienced in a particular way. Religious experience is not necessarily seeing some new thing (God, or an angel, or the Virgin Mary) in the same old way, rather it can be seeing very mundane things – books, buildings, common meals, the natural world – in a new way (Jones, 1971).

Augustine reads a religious text he has known for years and suddenly it grasps him in a new way. What changes? Not the words and lettering but his relationship to them. The eighteenth-century American theologian Jonathan Edwards is stupefied by the natural world as it suddenly appears "alive with the glory of God." What has changed? The trees, clouds, sky, grass are the same. But his relationship to them has been altered. In denoting something as sacred, the crucial thing is not the object but our relationship to it. And a crucial part of that sacralizing relationship is the idealization of the object. (This insight is the core of Martin Buber's philosophy which I discuss at length in Jones, 1991; 1996.)

Is everything idealized described as sacred? No. But, in contrast to Otto, who says that the experience of the sacred is *sui generis*, I would say that experiencing something as sacred is in continuity with other idealizing experiences, like romantic love or the ecstasy evoked by artistic perfection. This is what allows the language of love and the dynamics of music, painting, dance, poetry, and narrative to be carriers of the sense of the sacred. Focusing on the psychological category of idealization does not generate a theory of the experience of the sacred as unique and self-contained but rather produces a theory of how everyday objects and experiences become invested with sacred significance or become bearers of the experience of the holy.

Is this a complete theory of the sacred? Of course not. Like all psychological theories it focuses only on *psychological* factors. It says nothing about the content of the experience – Augustine's understanding of the nature of the divine command or Edwards' theology of divine sovereignty, for example – nor whether we should regard the cognitive claims that flow from such experiences as true. But it does underscore what I take to be one of the most elemental psychological dynamics in the religious life.

The further question of why some things become denoted and experienced as sacred and others do not may also lie beyond the boundaries of psychology. The psychologist can point out, as I have done here, that idealization is an important ingredient in the experience of the sacred. But that does not answer the question of why the ancient Celts apparently idealized certain trees, why Jews, Muslims, and Christians idealize certain books, why Roman Catholics idealize a certain institution, why Hindu and Buddhist practitioners of guru devotions idealize a certain teacher, and so on. Durkheimians answer this question by pointing to the connections between sacred objects and social organizations, i.e., ancient Celts lived close to nature, medieval Catholicism grew up in the legal and administrative ethos of ancient Rome. Such connections often exist, but to make a causal argument from the nature of society to the forms of a society's religion requires Durkheim's assumption of complete cultural determinism, and such a causal claim can run into difficulty when religions move from their culture of origin and flourish in a very different ethos.

Here again a more nuanced or dialectical understanding of the interplay of culture and subjectivity is probably necessary. Certainly the wider culture provides forms that are adopted by a religion. For example, the Roman empire provided the medieval Catholic Church with a hierarchical and legalistic view of institutional authority that was later taken into the Roman Catholic Church's ecclesiology and even theology. Thus the idealization of a religious institution and its authority. And Protestantism's "inner world asceticism" (Max Weber's term) fits neatly with the growing individualism and capitalism of the late Renaissance and early modern periods. Thus the idealization of a sacred book and the individual conscience.

Here again the insinuation of a certain cultural ethos into the realm of child-rearing and then the internalization of that family ethos (of, say, authority and submission or rational control of emotion) as a part of development produces a certain "social character." Thus formed, the person finds that such a social ethos seems natural and feels right. However, that is not the whole story. For the person may becomes conscious of how they have been impacted by their cultural ethos and may choose to reconstruct its inherited meanings and act differently. Thus religions and their adherents have not only echoed the *status quo* but have also challenged and reformed it. Like the relationship of the individual and culture, the relation of a religion to its culture is more nuanced and dialectical than Durkheim's social determinism allows. Such social determinism fails to give a full account of the power and diversity of religious idealizations.

Chapter 4

Idealization and religious fanaticism

A new experience of idealization can have a profoundly transforming effect as anyone who has ever experienced the ecstasies of falling in love knows. The author of the Song of Songs says being with his beloved makes him feel greater than a prince ruling over a myriad of subjects. "I met this woman and now I am a new man," a patient once said to me in a way that echoes what religious devotees often say about meeting Jesus, or Krishna or a powerful spiritual teacher. Focusing on the role of idealization helps account for the transforming effects of the experience of the sacred which will be discussed in more detail in the next chapter.

This underscores the psychological continuum between religious transformation and other forms of transformation. A new selfobject experience (whether idealizing, mirroring, or twinship) is bound to be transformative: powerful affects can be evoked, new possibilities of emotional investment can be opened up, new outlets for psychological energy can appear, new ways of experiencing oneself may be revealed. People feel new, become energized, look different, write poetry for the first time.

IDEALIZATION AND RELIGIOUS INFANTILIZATION

The question is not whether such experiences (religious or otherwise) are transformative (the dynamics of which we will discuss in the next chapter) but rather whether the transformation they evoke lasts. Kohut's theory of the developmental trajectory of idealization provides one way of answering that question. If the experience of falling in love, religiously or interpersonally, only serves to evoke an archaic emotion and does not provide any possibility of transmuting internalizations, then it will only keep the person in an infantile, object-hungry and addictive state.

But if the relationship with the beloved, religious, or interpersonal object allows its shortcomings to be acknowledged, its failures recognized, and its limitations supportively worked through – something few religious institutions seem to be able to do – then there is the possibility for genuine transformation towards maturity. If a church can acknowledge its errors, a guru admit his/her human failings, an expositor point out where a sacred text is mistaken, a teacher acknowledge where a meditational or ritual process has not worked, then transmuting internalization and increased self-cohesion is possible as the result of continued religious involvement. However, examples of such transformative realism and humility seem to me all too rare in the history of religions. Religions seem to require idealization as a prerequisite for commitment. And idealization certainly does evoke commitment and the investment of emotion. But then, if de-idealization occurs, religious commitment tends to weaken. Perhaps because they attract those prone to splitting and to over-idealization, religions seem to find it difficult to maintain both vital involvement and a realistic view of themselves. We will consider if this must be so in the last chapter.

If a religious institution insists it is pure and without error; if expositors insist that a text is infallible; if a teacher or master insists he or she is perfect, then the devotees will be kept in a state of developmental arrest, no matter how deeply they love that institution, or that text, or that teacher, or how powerful the emotions are that are evoked. In the final chapter we will return to the question of whether religious institutions and leaders must idealize themselves and their message, cloaking them in the garb of infallibility and perfection. This insistence on perfection and infallibility can contribute to splitting and the maintenance of object-hunger and immature dependencies, and it seems to me to be more often the rule, and not the exception, in the history of religions.

Many of the psychological problems with religion traditionally noted by psychoanalytic critics from Freud onward build on variations of this claim that religions keep people infantilized. For Freud, religion is inevitably infantilizing because it builds on and reinforces the child's dependence on an all-powerful father. To Freud, no other form of religion was conceivable (Jones, 1996). From a Kohutian standpoint, infantilization results when religious institutions and leaders keep their followers in a state of developmental arrest, playing on peoples' needs for over-idealization by presenting themselves and their message as perfect. Unless one is allowed an awareness of a religion's shortcomings, a realistic assessment and transmuting internalization cannot take place. Such over-idealization may well maintain the moral defense of splitting by which a person must experience themselves as debased in the face of a perfect being. A quick perusal of texts from many different traditions will reveal how often devotees are called upon to denigrate themselves in the face of some idealized reality. Thus a religion's overvaluation of itself may prevent transmuting internalization and mature object relations from developing.

Other psychologists of religion beside Freud have made a similar point about the pernicious effects of religious idealization and the splitting and abasement resulting from it. For example, Erich Fromm in a classic work published in 1950, *Psychoanalysis and Religion*, argues for the importance of religion and insists that "there is no one without a religious need, a need to have a frame of orientation and an object of devotion" (1950: 25). While devotion to an ideal and a source of meaning are essential to human life, Fromm builds his critique of religion on what he calls the dichotomy between "authoritarian and humanistic religion" (1950: 34). Authoritarian religion means "surrendering to a power transcending man" (1950: 35) while humanistic religion "is centered around man and his strength" (1950: 37).

Fromm has been roundly criticized by scholars in religious studies for this overly simple dichotomy which certainly does not do justice to the complexity of religious phenomena throughout human history (see, for example, Browning, 1975, for a sympathetic critique). But his main concern is elsewhere, with the psychodynamics of religious experience. Like Hartmann, Erikson, and Kohut, Fromm does not want to stigmatize all religion as psychopathological, and he criticizes Freud in this regard. Instead he wants to offer criteria by which to differentiate healthy from unhealthy forms of religion. For example, in writing about dependence he says,

> It is one thing to recognize one's dependence and limitations, and it is something entirely different to indulge in this dependence, to worship the forces on which one depends. To understand realistically and soberly how limited is our power is an essential part of wisdom and maturity; to worship it is

> masochistic and self-destructive. The one is humility, the other self-humiliation.
>
> (1950: 23)

Fromm's claim that worshiping a transcendental reality must be masochistic is certainly subject to critique. Numerous studies of conversion, for example, have shown that surrendering to a "higher power" can have positively transforming effects (Rambo, 1993). For example, this seems to be a major element in the healing process associated with Alcoholics Anonymous (Gorsuch, 1995; Galanter, 1989: ch. 9).

In a seminal article, the contemporary psychoanalyst Emmanuel Ghent (1990) argues for a distinction between "submission" and "surrender." Submission is more like what Fromm describes as masochistic and self-defeating whereas surrender (on Ghent's terms) involves the choice to give oneself over to a powerful aesthetic, romantic, or spiritual experience. On these terms, surrender is an essential aspect of any transforming experience. The inability or refusal to give oneself over temporarily to a powerful experience would certainly hinder a person's aesthetic enjoyment, sexual pleasure, or religious transformation and thus might itself be regarded as psychologically problematic.

Fromm's more basic assertion that religion can serve masochistic ends, however, seems very defensible. For example, in a rather polemical treatment of contemporary forms of authoritarian religion, Kathleen Ritter and Craig O'Neill (1996) present many clinical examples of the psychological ravages of the kind of authoritarian religion Fromm described. Elsewhere, I have described similar clinical examples of the pernicious psychological effects of authoritarian religion. A patient with a very masochistic personality with little self-confidence found his self-defeating style reinforced by a very rigid and controlling congregation. A young woman sexually molested by relatives as a child was forced to carry this secret alone because her church forbade talk about sex or communication with outsiders (Jones, 1995). I once had a patient tell me she belonged to a local church where the pastor taught that all independent thought came from the devil. If anyone questioned anything they were assumed to be demonically possessed. Such congregations seek to instill a habit of unquestioning submission in their members that can be socially dangerous and psychologically unhealthy, keeping their members in a state of passivity and dependence beyond that which is appropriate even for children.

Empirical research has also found strong correlations between certain types of religion and measures of authoritarianism, involving traits such as submission to authority, aggressiveness and hostility, conventionality, and closed-mindedness (a good review is found in Wulff, 1991). For example, one researcher in this field reports:

> Certain types of religious training appear to promote right-wing authoritarianism. [Such people report] that their religious training taught them to submit to authority more, led them to be more hostile toward "outsiders" and "sinners," and imposed stricter rules about "proper behavior," than do less authoritarian persons . . . So authoritarianism and certain types of religiosity appear to promote and sustain one another.
>
> (Altemeyer and Hunsberger, 1992: 115)

Summing up these studies of religious attitudes, Wulff writes in reference to certain rigid and controlling forms of religion that "researchers have consistently found positive correlations with ethnocentrism, authoritarianism, dogmatism, social distance, rigidity, intolerance of ambiguity, and specific forms of prejudice, especially against Jews and blacks" (1991: 219–20). Such conclusions from both clinicians and social psychologists are certainly in the spirit of Fromm's delineation of authoritarian religion.

Another classic text in the psychology of religion, Gordon Allport's *The Individual and His Religion* (1962), also attempts to distinguish mature and immature forms of religion. Although he does not focus directly on authoritarianism in religion the way Fromm does, Allport's analysis reaches similar conclusions. For him, maturity involves, at minimum, three characteristics: (1) self-control over biological impulses, (2) a self-critical perspective, and (3) a philosophy of life (1962: 53). Mature religion nurtures self-control, is self-critical, does not overvalue itself, and provides a unifying philosophy of life. Immature religion remains captive to selfishness and "impulsive self-gratification," is "unreflective" and uncritical, and "excluding, as it does, whole regions of experience . . . even when fanatic in intensity, it is only partially integrative of the personality" (1962: 54).

Crucial for Allport is the capacity to be self-critical or, to use his terms, to think in a way that is "differentiated" (1962: 58). He gives as an example two students talking about their fathers: the first describes her father as totally and completely perfect; the second describes her father as having positive but also negative qualities. Both like their fathers, but the second's viewpoint on her father is "more complex, more realistic" (1962: 59). Likewise, for Allport, the mature religious person maintains a differentiated, nuanced perspective on her religion.

He then raises a question we will return to at the end: Does this self-critical, realistic approach deprive religion of its zeal and passion? Is not "the absence of fanaticism in mature religion . . . a weakness?" he asks (1962: 65). His response is No. For him mature religion is what he calls a "master sentiment". It is the central organizing principle of a person's life, what the theologian Paul Tillich calls their "ultimate concern." Therefore,

> it characteristically keeps its ardor, and maintains throughout life an enthusiastic espousal of its objects, and an insatiable thirst for God. The degree of dynamism in the mature religious sentiment depends upon how central it is among all the various psychological systems that compose the personality.
>
> (1962: 65)

In other words, the immature person confuses fanaticism with devotion. The mature person realizes one can be deeply devoted to a religion, an ideal, a relationship, or a project and can make it central to one's existence and still maintain a complex and realistic perspective on it.

Another important characteristic, for Allport, of mature religion is its "functional autonomy" (1962: 63ff.). By this he means that religion is experienced as an end in itself and not used as a means to some other end such as gaining approval or respectability or pleasing others. Based on this construct Allport developed a category he called "intrinsic religion" and created a test to measure it. The immature or the "extrinsically" religious use religion in the service of something else: social conventionality, self-righteousness, ideological interests. The mature religious person is inner-directed, and her religion serves as an integrating "master sentiment" and source of meaning. Religion conquers selfishness and redirects lives to the extent that it is functionally autonomous and not in the service of narcissism.

From Freud to the present, psychologists have been concerned about the infantilizing effects of certain forms of religion. Some more sympathetic to religion than Freud, like Fromm and Allport, in their analysis of authoritarian and immature religion point to the same concern I have raised about the pathologizing and infantilizing effects of religious over-idealization and the concomitant authoritarian tendencies. Their analyses suggest, however, that religion does not have to be infantilizing or authoritarian – a conclusion we will reconsider at the end when we raise the question of whether there can be religion without idealization.

Such authoritarianism may, nevertheless, produce some healthy results. It is no accident that many drug addicts and criminals have been successfully rehabilitated by the black Muslims and very strict Christian groups, or very disciplined sects of Eastern religions. Such groups provide an external structure in which the self can function and grow when it lacks its own internalized structure. Often such groups provide the mirroring, idealizing, and twinship experiences that may have been lacking in their adherents' childhoods. Seen developmentally, such groups can perform an important function.

However, complete dependency on such structuring experiences is supposed to be temporary. Such experiences are to be internalized as self-structure and then the complete dependency on them outgrown. Most such religious organizations do not allow their converts to outgrow their dependency on these authoritarian systems. Rather than seeing such controlling measures as temporary, therapeutic expedients, adherents are encouraged to remain in this dependent state. If members do grow up, thanks in large part to the structuring experiences of the group, and seek appropriate adult autonomy, they are often forced to leave the group.

In the history of the psychological study of religion, it has proven much too easy to simply pathologize religions with which one disagrees. Certainly Freud, and to some extent Fromm, might well be guilty of that. Fromm's and Allport's analysis of authoritarian religion, however, is in the service of not simply debunking religion but rather generating diagnostic criteria by which the healthy aspects of religion can be separated from the unhealthy.

One such criterion, which nuances Fromm's otherwise overly simplistic analysis, is Ghent's differentiating surrender from submission which we will discuss in more detail in the next chapter. Surrender, in the non-masochistic sense, involves temporarily giving oneself over to effervescence generated by group dynamics, aesthetic power, sexual or other physical pleasures, or spiritual ecstasy. Masochistic and self-defeating submission, on the other hand, means remaining permanently and addictively dependent on an authoritative institution or leader.

Idealization (especially in the religious domain) is a profoundly ambivalent psychological process. Idealizing experiences can be powerfully transformative. They have the potential for restructuring the personality. But there are serious dangers here as well. By insisting on their own perfection, religious institutions, texts, and leaders may not allow for transmuting internalization to take place and so keep those devotees who are lacking in self-structure in a state of infantile dependence and object-hunger, thus producing the kind of authoritarian or immature religions that Fromm and Allport warned against.

There is another danger involved with idealization, especially in the religious domain, besides its fostering of immature dependency. I would suggest there is a connection between idealization and fanaticism, that religious fanatics tend to be those with highly idealized views of their religion.

IDEALIZATION AND RELIGIOUS FANATICISM

By fanaticism I do not mean simply orthodox belief within a Jewish, Christian, Muslim, Buddhist, Hindu or other tradition. The majority of orthodox believers and practitioners within these traditions are not religious fanatics in the sense I mean here. Nor do I want to use the category "fundamentalist" which is used by many of the authors cited in this chapter. Much of what I mean by religious fanaticism is also covered by the term fundamentalist as it is often used in scholarly and popular discussions. But I think there is a tendency to use the term fundamentalism to cover both orthodox belief and practice within a tradition and what I am calling fanatical religion whereas I want to distinguish them.

This is a very important point in considering this topic: separating orthodox belief and practice from fanaticism or "fundamentalism" (as it is often called). This distinction has been widely researched in the social-psychological literature. For example, one extensive study and review of the literature on this topic differentiates orthodox belief from "fundamentalism" by describing the latter as a closed-minded, ethnocentric and prejudiced system. "Fundamentalism," on this understanding is way of being religious rather than a specific set of beliefs. It is a way of holding and organizing traditional beliefs but it is not synonymous with those beliefs (Kirkpatrick, Hood, and Hartz, 1991). In this same vein, others have written,

> By "fundamentalism" we mean the belief that there is one set of religious teachings that clearly contains the fundamental, basic, intrinsic, essential, inerrant truth about humanity and deity; that this essential truth is fundamentally opposed by forces of evil which must be vigorously fought; that this truth must be followed today according to the fundamental, unchangeable practices of the past; and that those who believe and follow these fundamental teachings have a special relationship with the deity.
>
> (Altemeyer and Hunsberger, 1992: 118)

Studies of beliefs and attitudes using this type of definition find that those who approach religion this way are more likely to show tendencies towards violence and prejudice than those who simply held traditional beliefs. Such people "were more submissive [to authority] and more aggressive. And they were not more aggressive against just a few groups but against nearly all minorities" (Altemeyer and Hunsberger, 1992: 123, slightly altered).

In keeping with this social-scientific research, by "religious fanaticism" I here mean a militant style that involves splitting the world into good and evil and launching crusades against those perceived as "other," as evil. I am speaking about an aggressive form of religious intolerance. Not all who subscribe to orthodox or traditional beliefs within any religious tradition are "fanatics" in this sense. A point often lost in popular discussions of this issue.

While my focus here is on the psychological aspects of fanatical religions rather than their social and historical dimensions, two other characteristics of these combative religious movements are worth noting. First, such groups are often militantly nationalistic: seeing themselves as purifiers of their national or ethnic identities. And second, such groups are virtually always patriarchal in their social structure and their ideology: leadership is usually in the hands of men, the central texts are almost always composed by men, and women are usually taught to exist in a subordinate role. My concern here is with the psychological dynamic of idealization and what is idealized in such movements includes not only religious beliefs, practices, leaders, and institutions (which may also be true in non-fanatical but orthodox religious groups) but also ethnic and nationalistic symbols and often male dominance as well.

Consider the following quotations. The first is an amalgamation of several slogans from rabbis of the ultra-orthodox, nationalistic parties in Israel.

> The Land of Israel within its biblical borders has a lofty internal quality. Every bit of its territory, every clump of earth, is the holy of holies as the Torah declares . . . Redemption means sovereignty over the entire Promised Land . . . all weapons of the army which conquers and defends our land are of spiritual value and are as precious as religious articles. An IDF rifle and tank have the same value as the prayer shawl and phylacteries; soldiers are as important as Talmudic scholars, and settlers are a particularly saintly group.
>
> (Aran, 1991: 291)

An early spokesman for one of the national Hindu parties in India wrote the following around the time of Indian independence regarding other religious groups and those of non-Indian descent,

> There are only two courses open to the foreign elements, either to merge themselves into the national race and adopt its culture or to live . . . [in] the country at the sweet will of the national race . . . the foreign races . . . must lose their separate existence . . . or may stay in the country, wholly subordinated to the Hindu Nation, claiming nothing, deserving no privileges, far less any preferential treatment – not even citizen's rights.
>
> (quoted in Gold, 1991: 566)

It was his descendants that would later attack mosques, burn churches, and start riots in the name of purifying India and restoring what they considered traditional Hindu practices.

A similar marriage of nationalism and religion can be found among some of the Theravada Buddhists of Sri Lanka.

> Young Buddhists of Asia! The time has come for you to prepare yourself to enter the battlefield of truth, love and service . . . Arise, awake, unite and join the Army of Holiness and Peace and defeat the hosts of evil.
>
> (quoted in Swearer, 1991: 638)

The hosts of evil are, of course, the Tamil population of Sri Lanka, and there have been decades of bloodshed between the groups, often incited by their respective religious leaders.

This merging of idealizations – both of religion and of nationalistic and ethnic symbols – appears at the heart of fanatical religions and the crusade mentality that characterizes them. Not only are religious beliefs and practices idealized but there is often an idealized vision of one's national or ethnic group past or present.

For example, in his speeches, Randall Terry, spokesman for one of the most militant and violent anti-abortion groups in the United States, refers not only to religious and moral authority but also to an idealized and purified view of America's past.

> America must be "a nation where once again the Judeo-Christian ethic is the foundation of our politics, our judicial system, and our public morality; a nation not floating in the uncertain sea of humanism, but a country whose unmoving bedrock is Higher Laws".
>
> [quoted in Ammerman, 1994: 152]

With this conjunction of an idealized nationalism and religion comes a sanctification of violence against the outsider or anyone perceived as a threat. Militant Hindu nationalists have burned mosques and churches. Militant Muslims have engaged in international terrorism in the service of the Palestinian cause. An ultra-orthodox Israeli nationalist has written,

> With the perfection of our military system . . . the perfection of the essence of our rebirth is evident. We are no longer considered to be only "the People of the Book." Instead we are recognized as "the People of God," the holy people, for whom the Book and the sword descended together from heaven.
>
> (quoted in Don-Yehiya, 1994: 271)

The crusade mentality that is the core of what I mean by religious fanaticism seems to arise out of the merger of such idealizations of religion and tribe with the tendency towards splitting we discussed earlier in conjunction with Fairbairn's "moral defense." One commentator on fanatical religions has written that such groups "paint the world in black and white, creating radical polarities between good and evil" (Ammerman, 1994: 155). This splitting means that coming into the presence of an idealized object (a nation, a book, a teaching) demands that one must debase oneself. One way of dealing with that debasement and the painful feelings it evokes is to project them outward. Once this feeling of debasement is projected onto others, they become debased. They become subhuman, worthy only of extinction.

The demonizing of enemies is a major tactic of these fanatical religious movements. Khomeini proclaimed the West the "Great Satan." Shortly before his assassination I heard a group of ultra-orthodox rabbis on a New York radio station calling the late Israeli prime minister Rabin a traitor to the nation and an enemy of God who should be removed "by any means possible." Which, of course he was, when an ultra-orthodox Jewish student shot him. This demonizing of the other also requires a strict boundary between the group and the outside world and a drive for purity which Marty and Appleby take as a defining characteristic of the groups they studied, writing "fundamentalists set boundaries, protect the group from contamination, and preserve purity" (1991: 821). The pure must keep themselves totally aloof from the impure in order to preserve their purity and superiority.

The juxtaposition of these two themes in religious fanaticism – demonizing of the outsider and the ruthless purity of the insider – makes sense in terms of our earlier discussion of connection between idealization and splitting and the moral defense. The over-idealization of a nation, a tradition, a leader or a text can easily generate this rigid dichotomizing of life into the pure and impure which is such a central characteristic of fanatical religions. What one commentator rightly called, in reference to fanatical Muslims, the "tendency to bifurcate the world and deprive the faith of nuance" applies equally to all (Piscatori, 1994: 363).

In his study of fanaticism within Judaism, Christianity, and Islam, Lawrence (1989) sums up the importance of this splitting of experience and the idealization of one's group when he reports that one of the defining traits of such movements is that they

> are advocates of a pure minority viewpoint . . . [articulated] by charismatic leaders who are invariably male. Notions of a just social order in Iran, or a halakhic polity in Israel, or a Christian civilization in America [are] . . . to fundamentalists the necessary restoration of an eternally valid mandate.
>
> (1989: 100)

Whether it is a special definition of God-given borders in ancient Israel, or of a divinely approved Muslim state, or of a God-fearing American Christian commonwealth, certain convictions are elevated above all others and made the litmus test of the true believer. This drive for an exclusive claim to purity, divine approval, and eternal validity represents the idealizing tendency at work. Fanaticism is not simply orthodox belief within Judaism, Christianity, Islam, or any other religion, but rather orthodox belief tinctured with over-idealization of tribe and religion. White supremacists idealize a mythic and purified view of the Aryan race. The result is genocide against other races. Fanatical men idealize a patriarchal social order. The result is "honor killings" of women in Muslim countries and the burning of women in India and the witchcraft trials in medieval Europe.

Quoting Erik Erikson, Strozier (1994) carries this point further in his own study of religious fanaticism. Writing about the carnage that can result from such idealization and splitting within religion, Strozier says:

> A notion of a chosen people excludes everybody else, especially given the suffering outlined for these "others" in fundamentalist theology. As Erik Erikson observes: "While man is obviously one species, he appears and continues on the scene split up into groups . . . which provide their members with a firm sense of distinct and superior identity and immortality. This demands, however, that each group must invent for itself a place and a moment in the very center of the universe where and when an especially provident deity caused it to be created superior to all others, the mere mortals."
>
> Part of the power of Erikson's insight is the recognition that destruction between groups can only make sense with a spiritual grounding. We cannot value ourselves and degrade and ultimately kill the other unless we call God onto our side in the struggle. In the same way, the genocidal impulse is grounded in perverse forms of idealism and deep yearnings for spiritual purification.
>
> (Strozier, 1994: 252–3)

Idealization of one's own tribe, tradition, or gender in the name of religion provides a ready rationale for violence against the "other" who is now seen as demonic, impure, and thus available to be slaughtered with impunity. Much of the destruction wrought by religion arises from its idealizing tendencies in conjunction with the concomitant splitting that relegates the other to subhuman status, beyond the pale of empathic identification.

Erikson called this "pseudo-speciation," in which the single human race is split into ideologically driven subspecies by race or other external characteristics and then the groups are set against each other. For Erikson the most important point is that, in the words of Henry Stack Sullivan, "we are all more human than not." Pseudo-speciation obscures this fact by dividing this one human race into distinct racial, tribal, national, or ideological identities and attributing superior status to one group and inferior status to all others. Erikson provides a moving description of this process but little psychological account of it. Fairbairn's notion of the moral defense and Klein's discussion of splitting fill in this picture. This combination of idealization and splitting works against any drive to extend empathic identification and moral concern to those outside one's own group.

Idealization provides the psychological fuel propelling the missile of religious fanaticism. Such fanaticism, born of the devotee's overvaluation of some aspect of their own tradition – e.g. Israeli land, Muslim law, New Testament teaching, in the examples Lawrence describes – is (to me) one of religion's darker sides.

The theologian Reinhold Niebuhr makes a similar point about the ambiguity of religion in his discussion of social ethics entitled *Moral Man and Immoral Society*. Niebuhr was a major advocate of social justice in the United States in the post-World War II period. He felt that religion had played an important role in movements for social reform in the past and that it could continue to do so. Religion's main contribution to movements for social reform, according to Niebhur, was to provide the highest possible ideals and the motivation to strive to enact them. The problem was that religion's ideals were often so high that people either gave up trying to follow them or became fanatical in their pursuit of goals that could not possibly be achieved perfectly in an imperfect world. Religion, then, must provide ideals that are lofty enough that they are worth striving for but not so lofty that they can only engender fanaticism in the pursuit of them.

Idealization, then, is a crucial psychological dynamic in the denoting of a text, a person, an institution, or an experience as sacred. That idealization is a profoundly ambiguous process. From a self-psychological standpoint, objects of idealization are necessary to the development and maintenance of an active and energetic self. And Kohut and others have argued that religion is a primary source of appropriate objects of idealization. However, religious idealizations can be profoundly dangerous psychologically and socially. By insisting that their purity and truth are absolute, religions can split the world into camps of good and evil, can keep their adherents in a state of infantile dependence, and can generate a violent fanaticism. On the other hand, the encounter with an idealized, sacred object can be a profoundly positive and transforming experience, and we now turn to a psychoanalytic discussion of the transforming power of religious experience.

Chapter 5

Idealization and transformation

The last chapter examined some of the pathological dimensions of religious idealizations, particularly the infantilization of the faithful and the engendering of fanaticism. On the other hand, in different ways, Durkheim, Otto, Fromm, and Allport point to the tight interconnection between idealization and transformation. Now these connections need to be explored in more depth in order to develop a psychoanalytically informed account of the transforming power of religious experience. Traditionally psychoanalysts (from Freud, through Hartmann to Kohut, for example) have focused on the functional and adaptive (or non-adaptive) roles of religion. In this chapter I want to begin consideration, from a psychoanalytic standpoint, of the transforming impact of religion. Historically religions have not simply facilitated adaptation but have also led to the transformation of individuals and societies.

Consider the following accounts of religious experiences from two very disparate traditions and cultural contexts. In different ways, both illustrate the power of surrendering to experience within a religious context. The first is from the remarkable report of time spent with snake-handling Pentecostals by the Southern journalist Dennis Covington called *Salvation on Sand Mountain.* After many months of attending their services and visiting with them in their homes, one night Covington feels impelled to join the snake-handlers and pick up a huge timber rattlesnake. He writes:

> So the longer you witness it, unless you just don't get into the spontaneous and unexpected, the more you become a part of it. I did, and the handlers could tell. They knew before I did what was going to happen. They saw me angling in. They were already making room for me in front of the deacons' bench . . .

So I got up there in the middle of the handlers. [J.L.D], dark and wiry, was standing on my right; a clean cut boy named [S.F.] on my left. Who was it going to be? Carl's eyes were saying, you. And yes, it was the big rattler, the one with my name on it, acrid-smelling, carnal, alive. And the look in Carl's eyes seemed to change as he approached me. He was embarrassed. The snake was all he had, he seemed to say. But as low as it was, as repulsive, if I took it, I'd be possessing the sacred. Nothing was required except obedience. Nothing had to be given up except my own will. This was the moment. I didn't stop to think about it. I just gave in. I stepped forward and took the snake with both hands. Carl released it to me. I turned to face the congregation and lifted up the rattlesnake towards the light. It was moving like it wanted to get up even higher, to climb out of that church and into the air. And it was exactly as the handlers told me. I had no fear. The snake seemed an extension of myself. And suddenly there seemed to be nothing in the room but me and the snake. Everything else had disappeared. Carl, the congregation, Jim – all gone, all faded to white. And I could not hear the earsplitting music. The air was silent and still and filled with that strong, even light. And I realized that I, too, was fading into the white. I was losing myself by degrees, like the incredible shrinking man. The snake would be the last to go, and all I could see was the way its scales shimmered one last time in the light, and the way its head moved from side to side, searching for a way out. I knew then why the handlers took up serpents. There is a power in the act of disappearing; there is victory in the loss of self. It must be close to our conception of paradise, what it's like before you're born or after you die.

(Covington, 1995: 168–70)

The second account comes from Sogyal Rinpoche's *The Tibetan Book of Living and Dying*, in which this master of the Tibetan tradition seeks to explain his practice to Westerners. He describes the meditative state at the heart of his work as follows:

Rest in natural great peace.

Above all, be at ease, be as natural and spacious as possible. Slip quietly out of the noose of your habitual anxious self, release all grasping, and relax into your true nature. Think of your ordinary, emotional, thought-ridden self as a block of ice

> or a slab of butter left out in the sun. If you are feeling hard and cold, let this aggression melt away in the sunlight of your meditation. Let peace work on you and enable you to gather your scattered mind into the mindfulness of Calm Abiding, and awaken in you the awareness and insight of Clear Seeing. And you will find all your negativity disarmed, your aggression dissolved, and your confusion evaporating slowly, like mist into the vast and stainless sky of your absolute nature . . .
>
> What does this state feel like? Dudjom Rinpoche used to say, imagine a man who comes home after a long hard day's work in the fields, and sinks into his favorite chair in front of the fire. He has been working all day and he knows that he has achieved what he wanted to achieve; there is nothing more to worry about, nothing left unaccomplished, and he can let go completely all his cares and concerns, content, simply to be . . .
>
> Sometimes when I meditate, I don't use any particular method. I just allow my mind to rest, and find, especially when I am inspired, that I can bring my mind home and relax very quickly. I sit quietly and rest in the nature of mind; I don't question or doubt whether I am in the "correct" state or not. There is no effort, only rich understanding, wakefulness and unshakable certainty. When I am in the nature of mind, the ordinary mind is no longer there. There is no need to sustain or confirm a sense of being; I simply am. A fundamental trust is present. There is nothing particular to do.
>
> (Sogyal Rinpoche, 1992: 63)

Obviously these experiences are dissimilar in many ways. Covington's experience occurred in an intensely emotional group setting. Rinpoche's experience was solitary and calm. The Pentecostal experience seems to be spontaneous while the Tibetan experience is the result of years and years of disciplined practice. As a corollary, the Pentecostal experience is described as transitory and in need of being ritually re-evoked again and again while Buddhist practice aims at a continuing change in an individual's perception and cognition.

But these differences should not be exaggerated. Covington spent many months attending Pentecostal services before he was able to give himself over completely. Ritual participation might well be regarded as a spiritual practice. This too is an important point for the psychology of religion, which, since William James, has tended to focus on discrete and relatively short-lived moments when studying religious experience. James (1982) even said that "transitoriness" was one of the defining characteristics of a religious experience. Since James the psychology of religion has so often been the psychology of religious experiences. But in every major tradition such momentary experiences are a part of an ongoing series of practices: meditation, singing and dancing, studying texts, engaging in rituals. The spiritual life is not a series of atomistic ecstasies but rather a continuous pattern of disciplines and practices (a point which I stress in a more popular vein in Jones, 1995).

In addition, while Buddhist practice certainly intends the modification of an individual's fundamental structures of experience, Pentecostals report that the sense of the presence of the Holy Spirit "abides" with them long after the singing and prophesying and snake-handling have ended for the night. They do not regard their awareness of the Spirit's presence as necessarily fleeting or transitory.

And while Covington says clearly that his willingness to trust the group was an important factor in his being able to surrender to the ecstasy of the moment, Rinpoche also stresses time and time again that trust in a spiritual teacher or guide is necessary for a full realization of the meditative state. (Besides Soygal Rinpoche's book, Mark Finn (1992) also emphasizes the centrality of the relationship to the teacher in Tibetan Buddhism.) So the group effervescence of Pentecostalism and the solitary enlightenment of Tibetan Buddhism are both profoundly relational experiences. A point we will return to shortly.

How is it, from a psychoanalytic standpoint, that surrendering to experience in a religious context can be so powerfully transformative? The British pediatrician turned analyst D. W. Winnicott and the American analyst Hans Loewald both provide psychoanalytic discussions of religious transformation.

WINNICOTT AND HIS FOLLOWERS ON RELIGION

As we discussed earlier, Winnicott begins his theorizing from what he calls "a third area of human living, one neither inside the individual nor outside in the world of shared reality" (1971: 110). This "intermediate area of experience" begins with play in which the child "invests chosen external phenomena with dream meaning and feeling" (1971: 51).

Winnicott uses Freud's term "illusion" to name this intermediate psychological space.

> I am therefore studying the substance of illusion, that which is allowed to the infant, and which in adult life is inherent in art and religion, and yet becomes the hallmark of madness when an adult puts too powerful a claim on the credulity of others, forcing them to acknowledge a sharing of illusion that is not their own. We can share a respect for illusory experience, and if we wish we may collect together and form a group on the basis of the similarity of our illusory experiences. This is a natural root of grouping among human beings.
>
> (1971: 3)

Winnicott's use of the term illusion may create some semantic confusion. Winnicott's usage is vaguer than Freud's (1964) carefully delineated sense of illusion as involving wish-fulfillment. Thus, Winnicott finds it hard to remove the connotations of unreality and subjectivity that cling to the term illusion (Leavy, 1988; Loewald, 1988).

Winnicott is trying to reframe illusion from a synonym for error into a source of truth by making it synonymous with creativity and insight. The infusion of meaning from the inner world into actions and objects in the public sphere and/or the expression of inner-generated truths by means of external physical and verbal forms, describes not only children playing with teddy bears and empty boxes but also the creation of symphonies, sculptures, novels, and scientific theories, for "cultural experience [is] an extension of the idea of transitional phenomena and of play" (1971: 99).

Having moved from the world of pure subjectivity into a less responsive external world, Winnicott portrays the self as forever caught in the tension of inner and outer and struggling to relate his or her personal longings and insights to the unresponsive "not-me world of objects." Thus, the need to transcend the dichotomy of inner and outer, subjective and objective, lives on long after the teddy bear has been forgotten.

> The task of reality-acceptance is never completed, that no human being is free from the strain of relating inner and outer

> reality, and that relief from this strain is provided by an intermediate area of experience which is not challenged (arts, religion, etc.). This intermediate area is in direct continuity with the play area of the small child who is "lost" in play.
>
> (1971:13)

In the transitional process, out of which creativity emerges, the tension between objectivity and subjectivity is at least temporarily overcome, and inner and outer worlds momentarily fuse and the person gets "lost" in the revelry. Pulling together his disparate thoughts on this subject, Winnicott writes,

> I have tried to draw attention to the importance both in theory and in practice of a third area, that of play, which expands into creative living and into the whole cultural life of man. This third area has been contrasted with inner or personal psychic reality and with the actual world in which the individual lives, which can be objectively perceived. I have located this important area of experience in the potential space between the individual and the environment. . . . It is here that the individual experiences creative living.
>
> (1971: 102–3)

For Winnicott human life is impoverished if deprived of access to the transitional realm. Moments of rapture and ecstasy are necessary times of psychic refreshment and rejuvenation and are the source of creativity, sanity, and a full human life. Teddy bears and blankets and other childhood "transitional objects" are put aside but the capacity to enter and re-enter that transitional consciousness where the subject–object dualism is transcended abides as the source of the "creative living first manifest in play" (Winnicott, 1971: 100).

The significance of Winnicott's work for understanding religious transformation lies here, in his insistence on the importance of cultivating this richness of consciousness. Religious experiences allow entrance again and again into that transforming psychological space from which renewal and creativity emerge. Rituals, words, stories, and introspective disciplines evoke those transitional psychological spaces, continually reverberating with the affects of past object relations and pregnant with the possibility of future forms of intuition and transformation.

In an important and relevant paper already alluded to briefly, Emmanuel Ghent (1990) builds upon another aspect of Winnicott's theorizing. Winnicott suggests that if the parents interfere with the infant's creative spontaneity by imposing their own will on the infant's play, the child develops a compliant persona. If this parental impingement consistently overwhelms the child's spontaneity, the child may lose touch with her creative core (or "true self") and completely identify with the compliant façade. This results in what Winnicott calls a "false self" organization (Winnicott, 1971; see also Jones, 1997b).

In order for new psychological growth to take place, the false self must be broken through. Ghent proposes that beneath the false exterior there is a drive to lay down the façade and/or have it penetrated (the sexual connotations here are intentional) so that the true self can be known. This he calls a longing for surrender, that is surrendering the false self for the sake of "the discovery of one's identity, one's sense of self, one's sense of wholeness, even one's sense of unity with other living beings" (1990: 111).

If, for a number of defensive reasons, the path of surrender is closed, then the longing for surrender may be perverted into what Ghent calls an act of submission in which one denies one's own desires and intentions and allows oneself to be overpowered by another. With submission, "one feels one's self as a puppet in the power of another; one's sense of identity atrophies" (1990: 111). In other words, one becomes masochistic, hence the subtitle of Ghent's paper "Masochism as a Perversion of Surrender" (1990: 108). The sexual penetration in masochism becomes a poor substitute for the penetration of the false façade and the knowledge of the true self.

For the adult who has lost touch with the true self, one way to recover it is through surrender, the putting aside of the false self. Surrender opens a way to encounter again the true self, the spontaneous act, the transitional space. Writes Ghent, "I have suggested also that in many people there is an impulse to surrender, perhaps in order to re-engage that area of transitional experiencing, the miscarriage of which impulse or longing appears as masochism or submission" (1990: 124). So, Ghent suggests that surrendering to experience (especially in a religious milieu) is transformative because the façade of false selfhood is (at least temporarily) put aside and the true, free, and spontaneous self is reawakened. Awakening the true self is itself a powerfully transformative experience: defensiveness is replaced by spontaneity and depletion gives way to what Winnicott calls "feeling fully alive."

A psychoanalyst and professor of literature, Christopher Bollas, deals directly with many of these same issues in a series of reflections on psychoanalysis, provocatively titled (in a phrase taken from Freud) *The Shadow of the Object*. Bollas reaches back to the earliest days of awareness, to

> the human subject's recording of his early experiences of the object. This is the shadow of the object as it falls on the ego, leaving some trace of its existence in the adult.
>
> (1987: 3)

For Bollas, our early experiences are not encoded primarily as internalized objects, images, and representations: "The baby does not internalize an object, but he does internalize a process derived from an object" (1987: 50). By "process" here he means interpersonally generated affects, feelings, and "senses."

> The internal world is not simply composed of self and object representations. . . . A child may endure an experience which is registered not through object representation but through an identity sense . . . A child may thus have a profound self experience without being able to link this being state to any one object . . . they yield, instead, identity senses and they therefore conserve the child's sense of self or sense of being.
>
> (1987: 110).

Since we are dealing with experiences occurring before the dawn of discursive thought, they are not recorded in words or mental representations but in more diffuse and affective sensibilities: "the object can cast its shadow without a child being able to process this relation through mental representations or language" (1987: 3). Bollas terms these primal "senses" the "unthought known."

All later feelings about self and world are built upon these experiences arising in the mother–child dyad. This relational matrix provides the catalyst for integrating primal experiences – bodily sensations, primitive sights and smells and sounds, pains and pleasures that are the precursors of thought – into a sense of self and other. Thus Bollas terms this most primary maternal milieu the "transformational object" because in it the child learns to transform experience into information about self and world.

> I wish to identify the infant's first subjective experience of the object as a transformational object and . . . address the trace in adult life of this early relationship. It is an identification that emerges from symbiotic relating, where the first object is "known" not so much by putting it into object representation but as a recurrent experience of being – a more existential as opposed to representational knowing . . . the mother helps to integrate the infant's being (instinctual, cognitive, affective, environmental) . . . the mother is experienced as a process of transformation.
>
> (1987: 14)

So potent is this primary transformational tie to the mother that it casts a long shadow extending throughout a person's life. In times of crisis, the person longs for a transformational object that can facilitate the integration of new experience. In moments of ecstasy, like that described in much religious literature, a new transformational object has been discovered in another person, an overpowering piece of music, an evocative text, or the awesomeness of nature.

> This feature of early existence lives on in certain forms of object seeking in adult life. . . . the quest is not to possess the object; rather the object is pursued in order to surrender to it as a medium that alters the self, where the subject-as-supplicant now feels himself to be the recipient of enviro-somatic caring, identified with metamorphosis of the self . . . The memory of this early object relation manifests itself in the person's search for an object (a person, place, event, ideology) that promises to transform the self.
>
> (Bollas, 1987: 14)

Not only in moments of ecstasy but throughout all of life, the search for the lost transformational object goes on. Here again the experience of surrender is central to the process of transformation.

While similar in some ways to Winnicott's (1971) notion of the "transitional object" there are important differences as well. Whereas Winnicott's transitional objects are eventually outgrown, the transformational object is never simply put aside. The transformational object may itself be transformed (from the maternal matrix into "a person, place, event or ideology") but it is not outgrown. Of course, as we noted earlier, for Winnicott (1971) the transitional *object* is put aside but the transitional *capacity* to experience in an imaginative and fruitful way continues to mature and develop and forms the basis of creativity and culture. Winnicott often refers to this capacity as the ability to enter "the transitional space" – a state of consciousness which goes beyond the usual dichotomy of subjectivity and objectivity. In this sense Bollas's transformational object and Winnicott's transitional phenomena are similar: both point to the creative capacity lying at the heart of both art and science.

The search for a transformational object is rooted not in deficiency but in the positive experience of the caretaking dyad, it represents neither an emptiness nor a lack of self-structure but rather the natural desire to recover and re-experience something positive and growth-enhancing. The ecstasy of romance, aesthetics, and religion become the potentially positive carriers of this necessary aspect of human experience.

> In adult life, therefore, to seek the transformational object is to recollect an early object experience, to remember not cognitively but existentially – through intense affective experience – a relationship which was identified with cumulative transformational experiences of the self. Its intensity as an object relation is not due to the fact that this is an object of desire but to the object being identified with such powerful metamorphoses of being. In the aesthetic moment the subject briefly re-experiences, through ego fusion with the aesthetic object, a sense of the subjective attitude towards the transformational object.
>
> (1987: 17)

Bollas's discussion of the transformational object obviously resonates with many of the themes we have been discussing, especially when he writes, "the anticipation of being transformed by an object . . . inspires the subject with a reverential attitude towards it . . . the adult subject tends to nominate such objects as sacred" (1987: 16–17). The encounter with the sacred re-engages the self's fundamental experience of being constituted as a self in the psychological womb of the transforming object. The power of the sacred is, in part, that it carries the potential of recapturing the psyche's moment of creation and with it the promise of present and future moments of re-creation. (Another discussion of Bollas's work in relation to the psychology of religion can be found in Shafranske, 1992.)

This suggests that encounters with the sacred are almost inevitably experiences of transformation. Experiences of the sacred carry us back to and put us in touch with the foundations of our being and knowing – the transformational object. Such transforming moments are not simply memories of past events but rather represent a return to the foundational experiences of psychological life. They re-engage the wellspring of our conscious existence and carry the hope and the possibility of metamorphosis, of reworking or transforming aspects of ourselves and our relation to the world.

Such experiences point both backward and forward: back to a more primal (perhaps the most primal) state of consciousness; forward to new levels of integration and transformation by recreating the milieu which is the psychological catalyst of transformation.

By rooting the experience of the sacred in the most basic of human dynamics, Bollas implies that everyone has the potential for transformative, sacred experiences. The search for the transformational object or experience is not a neurotic response to life. Rather it is a continuation of the primary experience that constitutes and reconstitutes the self. Not a regression to an infantile state, the search for transformation is rather a part of the ongoing process of human development.

> We have failed to take notice of the phenomenon in adult life of the wide-ranging collective search for an object that is identified with the metamorphosis of the self. In many religious faiths, for example, when the subject believes in the deity's actual potential to transform the total environment, he sustains the terms of the earliest object tie within a mythic structure.
>
> (1987: 16)

All people have the potential to re-experience the moment of psychic creation and the process of metamorphosis. But just as, psychologically as well as biologically, we were not created in isolation but in the matrix of relationship, so the need for growth and change drives for a transforming object-*relation* that will sponsor that change.

Any suggestion that the drive for the transforming experience is intrinsic to human nature entails that this drive must latch onto some object. The ubiquity and necessity of transformational objects means that this impulse must go somewhere. Bollas writes, "In secular worlds, we see how hope invested in various objects (a new job, a move to another country, a vacation, a change of relationship) may both represent a request for a transformational experience and, at the same time, continue the 'relationship' to an object that signifies the experience of transformation. We know that the advertising world makes its living on the trace of this object" (1987: 16). Depending on the type of object to which it becomes connected, the drive for the transforming object experience can take negative as well as positive forms (1987: 17). In cults, addictions, and abusive relationships the wish for transformation becomes linked to a destructive object relationship.

The primacy of the transforming object parallels Otto's insistence on the primacy of the experience of the holy. It might appear as if these theories point in opposite directions: Otto's towards the sacred as transcendent ("wholly other") and Bollas's towards the sacred as immanent. But we have seen that Otto's insistence that we experience God as "wholly other" is misleading. Otto is right to insist that the experience of the sacred is numinous and mysterious, but possibly wrong to attribute that to the sacred, as experienced, dwelling beyond experience, for we cannot, within human experience, encounter what is intrinsically beyond human experience.

I suggested in my discussion of Otto that his most important contribution may be to insist that the sacred or holy is not itself an object of experience but is rather a characteristic of certain types of experience. The "numinous" cannot be an object of direct experience if it is a reality beyond experience. But numinosity, "awefulness," profound mysteriousness, can all be characteristics of certain experiences that we do have – experiences of nature, of sacred objects, of our own states of consciousness. The experience of the holy may not be a direct experience of an object called "the holy" but rather may be the experience of texts, natural wonders, charismatic individuals, ecstatic states, in an encounter filled with holiness, numinosity, and transformation. What then might be the source, within experience, of this numinous and transformative quality that marks out the encounter with the holy and the sacred?

One possibility, suggested by Ghent is that this transformational quality comes from the release of the true self. Another suggestion is

Bollas's claim that the sense of numinosity comes from the ability to transform us by re-evoking the birth of the self, that primal transformation of experience into self-structure through the dyadic catalyst of the transforming object. Thus the experience of the sacred is inevitably the experience of a transforming relationship. It is felt as ineffable because the experience recovers a state existing before words came into use. The experience of the sacred has a transcendental, numinous quality because such experiences resonate with the primal, originating depths of selfhood, going back before the dawn of the discovery of speech.

Winnicott's discussion of the transitional space resembles Victor Turner's (1967) use of the term "liminality," which refers to "that which is neither this nor that, and yet is both" (Turner 1967: 99). Turner focuses on the social functions of "liminality," especially the creation of community. Those who enter the liminal state where social and intellectual distinctions vanish are bound together by the experience.

For Turner, ritual is especially important in the creation of liminality. In an article published shortly after his death, Turner (1986) specifically connects play and ritual in ways that bring his thesis close to Winnicott's. Opposing those who only see ritual's socially conservative function, Turner calls ritual a "transforming performance" (1986: 158). He specifically links the culture-creating power of ritual to its evocation of a liminal (or "transitional") state since "through its liminal processes [ritual] holds the generating source of culture" (1986: 158). Play too "is for me a liminal or limoid mode essentially interstitial, betwixt-and-between all standard taxonomic modes, essentially elusive" (1986: 169). The link of play and ritual explains their creative potential, for both "can be said perhaps to play a similar role in the social construction of reality as mutation and variation in organic evolution" (1986: 171).

Turner and Winnicott as well as Bollas and Ghent point to the transforming power of entering a liminal or transitional state of consciousness where the usual distinctions of inner and outer, subjective and objective, temporarily fade. All agree that religious experience can be a powerful agent of personal transformation. Here the false self is put aside (Ghent) and the psychological ground of creativity (Winnicott) and transformation (Bollas) re-engaged. This re-evoking of the true self, of the spontaneous and creative moment, of the transformational object, makes such ecstatic states which are a central part of religious practice so psychologically powerful.

LOEWALD AND THE POWER OF RELIGION

A rather different account of the power of religious experience can be found in the writings of Hans Loewald. For Loewald, like Freud, mental life begins with our instinctual or unconscious nature, out of which higher mental processes – what Freud called "secondary process" – are generated. But the "primary process" must remain available to us. As opposed to Freud's attempt to keep id and ego, instinct and reason, in hermetically sealed compartments so that the purity of reason would not be contaminated by the irrationality of instinct, Loewald writes:

> There is no one way street from id to ego. Not only do irrational forces overtake us again and again; in trying to lose them we would be lost. The id, the unconscious modes and contents of human experience, should remain available. If they are in danger of being unavailable – no matter what state of perfection our "intellect" may have reached – or if there is a danger of no longer responding to them. . . . [we must find] a way back to them so they can be transformed, and away from a frozen ego.
>
> (1978: 22)

This cycle of mental development, arising out of the unconscious and returning to it again, reveals that the id, or what Loewald calls "the dynamic unconscious," is not simply the cause of neurosis as it was for Freud. The unconscious has a rationality all its own; Loewald says it is "a form of knowing, of 'minding'" (1978: 17). But it is a very different rationality from that employed by the ego in linear reasoning. One characteristic of the rationality of the unconscious is that dichotomies are transcended and a unity apprehended.

> If we acknowledge the undifferentiating unconscious as a genuine mode of mentation which underlies and unfolds into a secondary process mentation (and remains extant together with it, although concealed by it), then we regain a more comprehensive

> perspective – no doubt with its limitations yet unknown. Such a perspective betokens a new level of consciousness, of conscire, on which primary and secondary modes of mentation may be known together.
>
> (1978: 64–65)

Another major characteristic of the knowing generated by the primary process – besides a sense of unity – is a sense of timelessness. In moments of aesthetic, sexual, or religious ecstasy, our ordinary, linear sense of time is "overshadowed or pervaded by the timelessness of the unconscious or primary process" (1978: 67). Such "transtemporal" experiences point to a way of knowing that is "structured or centered differently, that beginning, and ending, temporal succession and simultaneity, are not a part [of such experiences]. They are transtemporal in their inner fabric" (1978: 68).

For Loewald, encounters with the dynamic unconscious are not unstructured eruptions of psychic chaos that disrupt for better (in the case of Julia Kristeva) or worse (in the case of Freud) the neat processes of linear reason. Like Loewald, Kristeva has a two-level theory of mind: what she calls the "semiotic" and the "symbolic." The "symbolic order" (a term shared with Jacques Lacan) is the domain of morality and culture. Paralleling Freud's view of civilization, the "symbolic order" is the social world that demands the renunciation of desire as the price of belonging. It is the patriarchal system built around the law of the father and his prohibitions. Beneath the "symbolic order" lies the "semiotic": a pre-linguistic reality having its origin in the infant's relationship to the mother and her body. The semiotic breaks forth in emotional states, dreams, and religious experience to disrupt the tidy world of patriarchal rationality (Kristeva, 1987). Such interruptions can represent psychosis and horrific distortions of life but they can also make space for creativity and art as well as mystical enlightenment. For Freud, of course, the intrusion of the unconscious is also disruptive; but, for Freud, that can only lead to psychopathology.

By contrast, for Loewald the dynamic unconscious is not unstructured or necessarily disruptive, unless the forms of rational consciousness are too rigid, as they often are in modern, excessively rational, individuals. Rather, the dynamic unconscious has its own structure, and encounters with it are, in William James's words, "noetic," bringing with them an authentic way of knowing the self and the world distinct from the knowledge gained by formal reasoning. Religious experience (for example) is, for Loewald, a genuine form of knowledge.

For Loewald "to be an adult . . . does not mean leaving the child in us behind" (1978: 21). Loewald rejects a one-way developmental street running from symbiosis to autonomy. A point emphasized by Nancy Chodorow (1989) in her treatment of Loewald. Rather, the drive for autonomy and the drive for merger continue side by side throughout the life-cycle. While psychoanalysis traditionally claimed that "the emergence of a relatively autonomous individual is the culmination of human development," Loewald writes, "there is a growing awareness of the force and validity of another striving, that for unity, symbiosis, fusion, merging, or identification – whatever name we wish to give to this sense of and longing for nonseparateness and undifferentiation" (1980: 401). This rejection of linear development in favor of a reciprocal model of the mind is a key characteristic of Loewald's theory: autonomy and merger, ego and id, consciousness and unconsciousness exist together within the individual rather than one being an outgrowing of the other. Maturity is not the relinquishing of experiences of merger and ecstasy but rather the capacity to move between ego and id, linear reason and primary process – states that exist side by side.

Our earliest mental state is not simply to be renounced, if not outgrown (as Freud thought), but rather to be returned to time and time again. Such returns are sources of creativity and refreshment. Loewald rephrases Freud's famous dictum "Where id is, let ego be" (that is, where irrational forces are, there should the rational ego be) when he adds "where ego is, there id shall come into being again to renew the life of ego and of reason" (1978: 16). Discursive reason alone renders human life sterile and flat. Conscious reason "limits and impoverishes" existence unless it has access to the more unitive and intuitive forms of knowing grounded in the dynamic unconscious. In words Freud could never have said, Loewald writes:

> the range and richness of human life is directly proportional to the mutual responsiveness between these various mental phases and levels . . . While [objective rationality is] a later development, it limits and impoverishes . . . the perspective, understanding, and range of human action, feeling, and thought, unless it is brought back into coordination and communication

> with those modes of experience that remain their living source, and perhaps their ultimate destination. It is not a foregone conclusion that man's objectifying mentation is, or should be, an ultimate end rather than a component and intermediate phase . . .
>
> (1978: 61)

The primary process with its complementary forms of rationality should be accessible even to the most highly developed intellect. Sanity consists not in renouncing the primary process but in remaining open to it. Loewald is thus an advocate of a far richer (than Freud's) vision of human experience – "a new level of consciousness, of conscire, on which primary and secondary modes of mentation may be known together" (1978: 65).

In reflecting on Freud's *Civilization and its Discontents*, Loewald argues that religion can be a primary carrier of this

> return, on a higher level of organization, to the early magic of thought, gesture, word, image, emotion, fantasy, as they become united again with what in ordinary nonmagical experience they only reflect, recollect, represent or symbolize . . . a mourning of lost original oneness and a celebration of oneness regained.
>
> (1988: 81)

Religious experience, then, can serve to keep us open to ways of knowing and being which are rooted in the primary process with its unitary and timeless sensibility.

> If we are willing to admit that instinctual life and religious life both betoken forms of experience that underlie and go beyond conscious and personalized forms of mentation – beyond those forms of mental life, of ordering our world, on which we stake so much – then we may be at a point where psychoanalysis can begin to contribute in its own way to the understanding of religious experience, instead of ignoring or rejecting its genuine validity or treating it as a mark of human immaturity.
>
> (1978: 73)

As we said before, for Loewald religious experiences are not simply unstructured eruptions of the unconscious, for "the experience of unity [with the primary process] is restored, or at least evoked, in the form of symbolic linkage" (1988: 45). This is possible because the dynamic unconscious is structured and religious symbols can carry or express this structure of timelessness and unity. If the primary process was simply chaotic, it could not be symbolized. Thus the dynamic unconscious gives rise to symbols and ritual actions which can express this structure in the conscious world.

Through symbols, ritual gestures, and other forms of expression, religion evokes a connection with the primary process in such a way that differentiation is not lost. We experience our relationship to the primary process in moments of timelessness and unity in such a way that we do not lose our capacity for secondary process (Loewald, 1988: ch. 4). Religious symbols and experiences are not purely the product of the unconscious (like a dream) or of objective consciousness but rather are influenced by both levels of the mind. Loewald is advocating neither living entirely out of the primary process, a "spaced out" (as my students used to say) life of continual merger, nor a life of frozen rationality alone but rather a life in which the "early magic of thought, gesture, world, image, emotion, fantasy" become united with ordinary experience. The life of religion in which symbols, rituals, altered states of consciousness, exist within institutions, philosophical systems, and moral teachings can exemplify this delicate dialectic.

Reformulating the primary process in more positive terms enables Loewald to speak for "the general validity or importance in human life of the different spheres and forms of experience" (1978: 71). Thus he can appreciate religious experience in ways that Freud – with his totally negative view of the primary process – never could. For Loewald religious experience is transformative in part because it enables us to know ourselves and the world in a new way – a way characterized by a sense of unity and timelessness in which our ordinary distinctions, differentiations, and sense of time disappear. This way of knowing is implicit in our nature but is seldom realized in our ordinary experience, especially in modern culture, which Loewald sees as too much under the hegemony of linear reason. In surrendering to experience in a religious context and thus re-evoking the dynamic unconscious, our perceptions of ourselves and the world around us are transformed.

WINNICOTT, LOEWALD AND THE PSYCHOLOGY OF RELIGION

We have looked at two parallel, psychoanalytic theories of religious transformation – Winnicott's idea of transitional phenomena and Loewald's reformulation of the primary process. There are certain differences between them. Loewald is critical of Winnicott's developmental model in which the infant is seen as moving from pure subjectivity into a world of objectivity. Instead Loewald describes the infant's world as a unique state of consciousness that exists before any differentiation of subjectivity and objectivity. (This difference is discussed in more depth in Jones, 1991 and Mitchell, 1998.)

Also Loewald focuses on a purely internal state as the analogue and source of religious experience: the dynamic unconscious or primary process with its transtemporal and unitive way of knowing. However, this unconscious is shaped by early interpersonal experiences. While existing as an intrapsychic domain, the unconscious originates in an interpersonal milieu of infant and parent, beginning from an "infant/mother . . . combination" (1988: 76). So Loewald too can be considered, in some sense, a relational theorist (Mitchell, 1998). Winnicott, on the other hand, consistently thinks in terms of an interpersonal realm of experience: an "intermediate area" fashioned from the infant's interactions. For Winnicott, even when experienced alone, the transformational state of consciousness is always a "between" rather than a "within," arising from the "potential space between the mother and the baby or joining mother and baby" (1971: 47).[1]

This difference between Loewald and Winnicott raises an important issue in the psychology of religion. Loewald's way of making psychoanalysis more open to religion by reconceptualizing the unconscious has a long history in the psychology of religion. It goes back at least as far as William James, who writes in *The Varieties of Religious Experience*,

> Whatever it may be on its farther side, the "more" with which in religious experience we find ourselves connected is on its hither side the subconscious continuation of our conscious life.

1 I am indebted to Daniel Berg (1997) for underscoring this difference between Loewald and Winnicott.

> Starting thus with a recognized psychological fact as our basis, we seem to preserve a contact with "science" which the ordinary theologian lacks. At the same time the theologian's contention that the religious man is moved by an external power is vindicated, for it is one of the peculiarities of invasions from the subconscious region to take on objective appearances, and to suggest to the subject an external control.
>
> (1982: 512)

Later, James writes, "we have in the fact that the conscious person is continuous with a wider self through which saving experiences come, a positive content of religious experience which, it seems to me is literally and objectively true as far as it goes" (1982: 515).

The major proponent of this baptism of the unconscious for religious reasons, of course, was Carl Jung, with his doctrine of the collective unconscious and the universality of archetypes. In ways very similar to James, Jung writes,

> I have often met with the objection that the thoughts which the voice [of the unconscious] represents are no more than the thoughts of the individual himself. That may be: but I would call a thought my own when I have thought it, as I would call money my own when I have earned it or acquired it in a conscious and legitimate way. If somebody gives me money as a present, then I will certainly not say to my benefactor, Thank you for my own money, although to a third person and afterward I might say: this is my own money. With the voice [of the unconscious] I am in a similar situation. The voice gives me certain contents, exactly as a friend would inform me of his ideas. It would be neither decent nor true to suggest that what he says are my own ideas . . . Someone may object that the so-called unconscious mind is merely my own mind . . . but I am not at all certain whether the unconscious mind is merely my mind, because the term unconscious means that I am not even conscious of it.
>
> (Jung, 1938: 46)

For Jung, like James, the unconscious is greater than the individual ego and we do not know its boundaries. The unconscious, according to this line of thought, might very well be infinite and could easily represent the infinite to which religion often points.

Loewald does not go as far as Jung in transforming metapsychology into metaphysics, but like Jung he both roots religious experience in the unconscious and reframes the unconscious into a source of healing and wisdom.

The first move, rooting religion in the unconscious, goes back to Freud as well as James. In the critique of religion undertaken by Freud and other classical analysts, religion is simultaneously debunked and also transformed into a kind of psychology, that is, made another window on the unconscious. For example, for Freud in *The Future of an Illusion*, religious beliefs provide the analyst with insight into the nature of infantile narcissism and its refusal to accept the realities of death, nature, and social constraint. Religion is a direct expression of the reality-denying wishes of the id. This revisioning of religion into a tacit form of psychology is possible for Freud because of the close connection of religion and the unconscious or id.

The difference over religion between Freud and classical analysis on one hand and Loewald and Jung on the other derives not from a theoretical rooting of religion in the unconscious (a move they all share) but rather from their radically different understandings of the unconscious. For Freud and his followers, the unconscious is a cauldron of antisocial drives and infantile wishes; experienced directly the id can only be a source of psychopathology. So connecting religious experience so closely to the unconscious makes it seem necessarily pathological. For Jung, on the other hand, the unconscious is a source of greater wisdom and healing, and for Loewald it is the source of a crucial mode of knowing the world. So for Jung and Loewald, religion, with its connection to the unconscious, represents a major mode of healing and a vehicle for authentic and transformative knowledge.

Such an approach has the advantage, as James points out, of remaining in continuity with a recognized element in psychoanalytic theory – the unconscious – while conceiving of it in rather untraditional ways. Such a move foregrounds an immanent source for religious experience while providing a psychological reason for the experienced sense of a power transcending the individual ego. And (in the case of James and Jung, at least) this position remains open to the possibility of a reality altogether transcending the physical world. But with James and Jung a kind of psychological ontology is created in which the unconscious becomes the universal ground from which individual selfhood emerges. We have here a theology in psychological dress. James's and Jung's model is structurally like a theology in that it claims there is a power transcending the individual ego which brings healing and wholeness, that we cannot transform ourselves by reliance of ego rationality alone, and, in addition, they offer new objects of belief (like the collective unconscious).

Winnicott's rapprochement with religion, on the other hand, remains within the domain of epistemology; he proposes no new realities like Jung's collective unconscious or James's "higher power." Rather he suggests in his epigrammatic way that there exists a third area of knowing which is neither purely objective nor totally subjective into which religion (as well as art) falls. This "intermediate area of experience . . . is not challenged" (1971: 13). But that does not mean it cannot be shared. "If, however, the adult can manage to enjoy the personal intermediate area without making claims, then we can acknowledge our own corresponding intermediate areas, and are pleased to find a degree of overlapping, that is to say common experience between members of a group in art or religion or philosophy" (1971: 14).

Freud and many contemporary positivists think of science as totally different from the knowing found in art, religion, or philosophy. They envision a strict dichotomy of reason and imagination. However, a more nuanced and contemporary philosophy of science suggests that all knowledge is transitional and interactional in Winnicott's sense. In science too discursive reason and imaginative creation interpenetrate. Pragmatic realities constrain imaginative reconstructions, while creative reinterpretations reframe empirical experience. No precise line can be drawn between objective and subjective spheres or between the products of reason and imagination (Jones, 1992, 1996, 1997, 1999). Newton's (perhaps apocryphal) drawing a connection between a falling apple and the force that maintains the planets in motion around the sun, or Einstein's seeing a way to represent geometrically Newton's gravitational force and the structure of the universe, were tremendous imaginative leaps. The same is true of Bohr envisioning the atom as a tiny solar system and DeBrogli re-envisioning it as a series of waves. Without such creative imaginings, we would still be practicing Aristotelian physics.

Yet such imaginative leaps are hardly irrational. Each enabled scientists to make sense of new domains of experience and experimental data. Each generated radically new ways of reasoning and of conceptualizing the world – Newton's celestial mechanics, Einstein's general relativity, contemporary quantum mechanics. Such scientific models and paradigms as Newtonian mechanics or general relativity are neither purely objective nor subjective (Arbib and Hesse, 1986; Lakoff and Johnson, 1980).

A "transitional" (in Winnicott's sense) way of knowing is equally characteristic of natural science, psychoanalysis, and religion. Winnicott's approach to religion offers no new objectives of belief (such as archetypes or universal minds) but rather a different way of thinking about the epistemological status of more traditional religious beliefs. The attempt to use Winnicott to reconstruct the epistemological status of religious claims has become a major feature of the contemporary psychoanalytic discussion of religion. In different ways authors like Meissner, Rizzuto, Pruyser, and myself have argued that religious beliefs and practices can be understood as "transitional phenomena" in Winnicott's sense: neither purely subjective nor completely objective (Jones, 1996).

In a way Loewald spans both the quasi-ontological approach of James and Jung and the epistemological approach of Winnicott. In linking religion to the unconscious, Loewald too reframes the unconscious into something positive and "higher" (in some sense), but what emerges from the unconscious is a new way of knowing: self and world experienced as unified and timeless.

The epistemological approaches of Winnicott and, to some extent, Loewald address the psychological quality of religious experience but not its content. Religious experiences, whatever their content, are valued when they evoke the transitional realm or give us renewed access to the dynamic unconscious. But their cognitive content is bracketed off. The quasi-ontological approach of James and Jung offers a psychological alternative, or at least complement, to the content of traditional religious beliefs – James's universal mind or Jung's collective unconscious. The epistemological approach of Loewald and Winnicott is an alternative way of viewing religion but it is not, in any way, an alternative religion. Quite the reverse: it depends on traditional religions to supply content to its analytic categories like transitional experience or dynamic unconscious. Jung and James, on the other hand, propose new objects of belief that might compete with the contents of more traditional religious creeds. They create something that is neither a religion nor a psychology as traditionally conceived but is more like a type of synthesis of both. It is a kind of psycho-theology.

While Loewald speaks of a new way of knowing, the difference between him and Winnicott here reflects two approaches in the history of the relationship of psychoanalysis and religion and the possible rapprochement between them. Loewald establishes such a reconnection through the more inward-directed avenue of redefining the nature of the unconscious, following in the footsteps of James and Jung. Winnicott suggests that human experience is too complex to fit entirely within the modern dichotomy of subjectivity and objectivity, internal and external, and that there is a third epistemological domain, which is not reducible to either, to which religion belongs. For Winnicott religion is not a totally inward and individual reality as it is for James and Jung and perhaps Loewald, arising wholly out of the depths of the unconscious. Rather Winnicott's third area of knowing is relational and interactional, arising out of the child's creative interactions with the people and the physical objects in her early environment and later giving birth to the whole world of culture including art, religion, and science. As Winnicott writes, "I have located this important area of experience in the potential space between the individual and the environment. . . . It is here that the individual experiences creative living" (1971: 103).

These differences should not obscure those similarities between Loewald and Winnicott relevant to a psychoanalytic understanding of religious experience and its transforming power. Loewald and Winnicott both emphasize that human life is impoverished if it is lived wholly in the realm of "objectifying mentation." Linear rationality alone constricts life. Episodes that transcend objectivity are necessary for "the fully human life."

But religious experience is valued not simply as a supplement to rational living or as a momentary aesthetic release from the world of objectivity. Like William James, both Loewald and Winnicott see religious experience as noetic, that is it gives us an authentic knowledge of reality. It is not pure feeling (as Otto seems to suggest) but is rather a way of knowing. In religious experience what is transformed is both our way of knowing and what it is we know. For Loewald religious experience is a way of knowing ourselves and the world under the rubric of unity and timelessness. For Winnicott it is a way of knowing that gets beyond the dichotomy of subjectivity and objectivity in which he seems to feel we are trapped much of the time and enables us to enter that state of consciousness from which creative insights and intuitions arise.

Here Loewald goes beyond Winnicott. While struggling to get beyond the dualism of subjectivity and objectivity, Winnicott remains within this dichotomous thinking. Objective reason is understood in much the same way as Freud did (Jones, 1997). For Loewald reason itself must be transformed by continual reconnections with the dynamic unconscious and the forms of knowing found there. (For more on the epistemological implications of contemporary psychoanalysis, see Jones, 1992, and 1996.)

Both theories center on ecstatic experience. What role does idealization play here? Winnicott insists that a zone of safety is necessary to facilitate transitional experience which requires "a relationship that is found to be reliable" (1971: 47). The child can play freely and creatively, even when alone, because he or she has internalized the security provided by the parental relationship. Winnicott writes, "the potential space happens only in relation to a feeling of confidence on the part of the baby, that is confidence related to the dependability of the mother-figure or environmental factors, confidence being the evidence of dependability that is becoming introjected" (1971: 100). For Winnicott, then, an interpersonal context of trust and dependability is necessary for the invocation of transitional experience. An individual who is anxious or insecure cannot let go enough to enter the transitional sphere.

An idealized teacher, text, group (or therapist) may evoke enough trust that the person is able temporarily to weaken their normal ego boundaries and the grip of "objectifying mentation." Ghent writes about this in regard to the transforming power of surrendering one's ego,

> Because we are so impressed with our "ego," we need to find something or someone who so totally transcends our experience, whose presence is so totally affirming that we will take a chance on surrendering. Hence the guru, and in a different world, the analyst. He is an excuse, an ally for the true self to come forth.
>
> (1990: 112)

Several authors have written about the requirement of such trust in a teacher in order to experience the full transforming effects of Tibetan Buddhist practice (we have already mentioned Sogyal Rinpoche and Mark Finn in this regard). Covington also writes about how trust in the Pentecostal people he had come to know enabled him to move into their experience. He writes, "I figured I could trust my guide, I'd be all right. I'd come back to earth in one piece. I wouldn't really lose my mind. That's what I thought anyway . . . So I got up there in the middle of the handlers" (1995: 168). A trusting relationship with an idealized other seems to be an important facilitator of surrendering one's hold on objectifying reason. Such loosening of the constraints of normal, rational existence is necessary for entering into the transitional realm or reconnecting with the primary process – those psychological movements through which transformation takes place.

In different ways Winnicott and Loewald move away from Freud's (and other classical analysts') sole reliance on linear rationality and look positively on the potentially transforming impact of ecstatic religious experience like that described by Covington and Sogyal Rinpoche. Loewald goes so far as to write, "I believe it to be necessary and timely to question that assumption, handed to us from the nineteenth century, that the scientific approach to the world and the self represents a higher and more mature evolutionary stage of man than the religious way of life" (1980: 228). Linear rationality is not the only way to knowledge. The fully human life requires that discursive reason be supplemented and complemented by more ecstatic, unitive, and ineffable ways of knowing like those found in religious experience. And such experiences are usually catalyzed by the presence of an idealized other.

This openness to, and perhaps advocacy of, ecstatic and transforming religious experience represents a major departure in the psychoanalytic approach to religion. Such an alternative approach to religion parallels recent changes in the goals of psychoanalysis itself. Freud saw the aim of analysis as the sublimation and redirection of instinctual energy. The ego psychologists defined health in terms of adaptation and adjustment. Contemporary relational theorists like Winnicott, Loewald, Bollas, and others make creativity and self-realization the marks of the healthy self. Where Freud sought the renunciation of whole domains of experience in the name of rationality, many contemporary analysts seek to reclaim and recover equally large domains of experience in the name of creativity and authenticity (Mitchell, 1993). Sometimes, as with religion, the very experiences Freud called on his patients to renounce, contemporary analysts seek to restore. Whereas Freud spoke of resignation and rational self-control, Kohut, Winnicott, Loewald and others seek to revitalize the patient's capacity for experience. As the analytic focus shifts from instinctual control to the quality of experience, religion has a potentially more positive contribution to make to mental health. For Freud, religion can only serve as an agent of instinctual repression. For more contemporary theorists, religious traditions with their sophisticated cartographies of a variety of states of consciousness and their powerful techniques for evoking them, may have a singular role to play in human health (for example, Rubin, 1996). On the contemporary psychoanalytic scene, such ecstatic, trans-rational experiences and states of consciousness can become marks of wholeness, not signs of psychopathology.

Idealization and religious transformation are connected in several ways. Idealizing, selfobject transferences (in Kohut's sense), like romantic love, being awestruck by nature, or religious encounters, are almost always transformative. Falling in love or experiencing a "conversion" (in which an other or Other is idealized) can release new energies, renew creative abilities, restructure the personality. Such events can facilitate the creation of new psychic structures and restart arrested self-development. In addition, the presence of an idealized teacher or community can evoke the experience of trust and surrender through which the true self may be liberated and lost dimensions of the self rediscovered.

Chapter 6

Religion without idealization – is it possible?

Can there be religion without idealization? Religious fanaticism is a major problem in the world, so religion without idealization may be a major social need today. But idealization is also a major source of religious transformation. Does this entail that a religion without idealization is a religion without transformation, that is, is not really religion at all?

First, we should note that, while idealization is central to every religion, many religions also contain de-idealizing trajectories. "If you meet the Buddha on the road, kill him" is an oft-quoted Zen saying. And there is a common simile in Buddhism that compares the Dharma (the Buddha's teaching) to a raft: you use the raft to cross the stream, but once you arrive on the other side (enlightenment) the raft is discarded. So the practices and teachings of the religion are to be regarded as tools, means to an end, not as ends in themselves.

Another kind of religious de-idealization can be found in the Hebrew prophets. For example:

> I hate, I despise your feasts
> I take no delight in your solemn assemblies.
> Even if you offer me your burnt offerings and cereal offerings,
> I will not accept them
> And the peace offerings of your fattened beasts
> I will not look upon.
>
> (Amos 5.21–2)

Jeremiah warns his people not to keep intoning, "the temple of the Lord, the temple of the Lord" as though it were a magic charm that could ward off the coming calamity. In this way the prophetic voice in Israel worked against any tendency to idealize the temple, their ritual practices, and other such objects of devotion. And God's destruction of the kingdom of biblical Israel by the Assyrians and Babylonians can be read as the most radical de-idealizing event of all. For the promise of a kingdom had been central to Israelite faith since the days of Abraham, but the prophets said, God could and would bring an end to that most cherished ideal – their own land and government.

Jesus' statement that "the sabbath was made for man, not man for the sabbath" can be read in the same context. According to the Priestly tradition in Genesis chapter 1, the existence of the sabbath on which God rested was the goal and culmination of the whole process of creation. In that sense the sabbath stands for the entire divine order including Torah and temple. When Jesus says that humankind was not made to serve the sabbath, the law and the temple but rather the other way around, this too was a radical de-idealizing of religious teachings and traditions. The forms and institutions of religion, however divine their origin and sacred their significance – and there is no evidence Jesus questioned the divine origin of the sabbath or the law – are not to be taken as ends in themselves. Rather they exist to serve humankind, not the other way around.

Centuries after Jesus, the Protestant reformers condemned what they saw as the idolatry and absolutizing of the medieval church's sacramental worship and claims of divine authority. The Protestant reformers' constant polemic against idolatry can be read as another de-idealizing force within Christianity in the tradition of the Hebrew prophets and Jesus' teachings. The history of Christianity from Jesus' disputes with the Pharisees of his day through the reformers' attacks upon the medieval church are another example of the continual dialectic between tendencies towards idealization and de-idealization within the religious life.

Likewise with the mystics' apophatic insistence that the divine reality is beyond all human categories and so can only be experienced as a *via negativa*, a way of negation. For example, the *Tao Te Ching* opens with the saying, "The Tao that can be named is not the eternal Tao." A Westerner might also say, "The God that can be named is not the eternal God." In this tradition stands John of the Cross's description of the "dark night of the soul." Thomas Aquinas is reported to have said, in the face of a mystical experience, that all of his writings, the massive *Summa Theologica* and *Summa Contra Gentiles*, were like "straw."

The contemporary philosopher and theologian Paul Tillich (1957) writes of the dialectic between doubt and faith. Faith is necessary to connect us to the universal, primal ground of our existence. Doubt is necessary, lest the relative, finite, human structures of faith be absolutized and put in the place of God. In many ways this parallels the dialectic at the heart of Kohut's discussion of romantic love: enough idealization (faith) so we can be passionately invested in our beloved, enough realism (doubt) to keep our romantic passions and wishes grounded. So both idealizing and de-idealizing forces are not foreign to religious traditions themselves, including Judaism and Christianity, or only confined to religion's critics.

THE *VIA NEGATIVA*

A major de-idealizing dynamic within the religious domain can be found in the apophatic tradition. At the end of the fifth century an anonymous author known to us as Dionysius the Areopagite wrote a brief essay called the *Mystical Theology* premised on the claim that all human categories are limited and finite. To speak directly about God (either by affirming or by denying "Him") would limit God by treating God like an object in the world of tables and chairs. That is precisely what God is not. Since the divine is beyond all categories, God's existence can neither be affirmed nor denied.

> Neither is He darkness nor light, nor the false nor the true; nor can any affirmation or negation be applied to Him . . . We can neither affirm nor deny Him . . . [the] Cause of all things transcends all affirmation, and the simple pre-eminence of His absolute nature is outside of every negation – free from every limitation and beyond them all.
>
> (Happold, 1975: 217)

Neither theism or atheism can capture the truth about God, for "there is no contradiction between the affirmations and negations [of God] . . . being beyond all positive and negative distinctions" (Happold, 1975: 213).

Religious creeds, practices, traditions are built around certain images, ideas, or concepts that become idealized in the process of our fully investing ourselves in them. Each religious tradition is centered on specific core metaphors to which idealizing transferences are often attached as these claims are sacralized: "the ways of the Tao are effortless," or "reality is empty," or "the law of the Lord is just," or "God is love." Even the atheist clings to his or her concept of God whose non-existence he or she passionately defends. Passing through what another writer in this tradition calls "the cloud of unknowing" wrenches all these constructs away, leaving nothing to cling to, leaving no satisfactory way of speaking about, or arguing against, or grasping, any ultimate source of security. The contemporary Thomas Merton simply states, "In the deepest darkness we most fully" find God.

Inevitable limitations on human experience and expression mean that ultimately the divine can only be encountered (if at all) as the negation of all concepts. This tells us nothing about the nature of the Ultimate – which remains beyond our ken – but only that any encounter with God must finally pass beyond language into a state in which concepts disappear into a void.

Here we have to be exceptionally careful. The void is not another, more correct, image. It is neither atheism nor theism. Dionysius speaks of God as "beyond affirmation and negation." The void is precisely what cannot be reified into concepts because it is the experienced death of all concepts. The *via negativa* is not about having the correct understanding of the idea of emptiness or the correct concept of the void. It is about entering into the experience of the void. People may intellectually defend themselves against this experience of emptiness, of negation, by turning emptiness into a concept which can be discussed and debated and so protect believers from the actual encounter with pain and loss which the de-idealization of their cherished beliefs involves.

The *via negativa* is not a metaphysical statement about the nature of the divine. Rather it is a claim about the ultimate impossibility of any such statements, for "no affirmation or negation can be applied to Him." Instead of metaphysics or theology, the *via negativa* is a transformational strategy, a spiritual discipline. A process undertaken, not a theory propounded.

The fifth-century desert contemplative John Cassian wrote of three renunciations. The first is the renunciation of a person's old way of life, the way of life wholly devoted to selfish pursuits. This renunciation is the basis of any spiritual quest. The second is the renunciation of our attachment to our habitual thoughts. Through the practice of meditation, a detached perspective on our thoughts and desires gradually develops. This meditative practice too is a part of virtually every spiritual tradition (Funk, 1998). The third and final discipline is the renunciation of our idea of God, which a contemporary commentator describes:

> The third renunciation . . . is to renounce our very idea of God. Since God is beyond all images, thoughts and concepts, then we must renounce our cherished beliefs for the sake of loving God as God. This third renunciation is a natural fruit of years and years of prayer and meditation and/or God's gift.
>
> (Funk, 1998: 24)

Here the renunciation of the idea of God leads, paradoxically, to a deeper experience of God.

In the same vein, the fourteenth-century English spiritual classic appropriately called *The Cloud of Unknowing* says,

> It is usual to find nothing but a darkness around your mind, or, as it were, a cloud of unknowing. You will know nothing and feel nothing except a simple reaching out to God in the depths of your being. No matter what you do, this darkness and this cloud will remain between you and your God. You will feel frustrated, for your mind will be unable to grasp him. Learn to be at home in this darkness. Return to it as often as you can . . . If in this life you hope to feel and see God at all, it must be within this darkness and this cloud.
>
> (ch. 3)[1]

To know God is to enter a cloud, a darkness, where all knowing ceases.

Knowing ceases but love remains. Love takes up where thought has reached its limit.

> But now you put to me a question and say, How might I think of him in himself, and what is he? And to this I can only answer thus, I have no idea. For with your question you have brought me into the same darkness, into that same cloud of unknowing

1 In the quotations from *The Cloud of Unknowing* in this chapter I have worked with two translations, Johnston (1973) and Walsh (1981).

> where I wish you were yourself . . . No man can think of God himself. Therefore it is my choice to leave behind everything that I can think of and choose for my love that which I cannot think. For why: He may well be loved but not thought. He can be taken and held by love but not by thought.
>
> (ch. 6)

Here the author of *The Cloud* goes beyond the more intellectual approach of Dionysius in which discursive reason forces itself to its limits in order to encounter the darkness in which dwells "That Which transcends all affirmations" (Happold, 1975: 216). According to *The Cloud*, longing and love are necessary to reach where reason cannot go. "With a devout and a pleasing stirring of love, strive to pierce that darkness above you. You are to smite upon that thick cloud of unknowing with a sharp dart of longing love" (ch. 6).

Of course this is striking from a psychoanalytic standpoint. The author is talking about desire – "a sharp dart of longing love." He (all commentators assume the anonymous author is a man) begins, like Plotinus before him, with desire. Our natural desire is to enter into a conscious relationship with the source of our existence. There is no sense here of God as a controlling and overpowering force (as in Otto, for example). There is nothing here of the domineering power that can generate the moral defense with its splitting of the world into antagonistic camps of darkness and light. The author of *The Cloud* certainly speaks of evil and sin, but they are distractions that lure us from our true desire. They are to be met with loving techniques that enable us to detach ourselves from their power and refocus our attention (for example, chapters 10 and following).

God attracts, God does not coerce. Our natural desire for a loving union with our Source lures us forward. The longing for God is not opposed to our natural experience but rather rises up from within the domain of our desire. The spiritual life comes to us not primarily as duty or argument but as desire. The function of religious practices – "the lesson, the meditation, and the petition . . . [or] they may be called, for a better understanding, reading, reflecting, and praying" (ch. 35) – is to facilitate and shape desire. But this facilitation of desire through spiritual practice is not the heteronomous imposition of constraint against nature (as Freud thought of religion). Rather it is enabling desire to follow its deepest natural course and reach its most fulfilling end.

As part of the process of entering the cloud of unknowing, all other constructs must be put aside.

> If ever you come to this cloud, and live and work in it as I bid you, just as this cloud of unknowing is above you, between you and your God, in the same way you must put beneath you a cloud of forgetting, between you and all the creatures that have ever been made . . . I make no exceptions, whether they are bodily creatures or spiritual . . . whether these be good or evil.
>
> (ch. 5)

This applies not just to those objects unrelated to religion but even to those considered most spiritual.

> Therefore, though it is at times good to think of the kindness and worthiness of God in particular. And though this is a light and a part of contemplation, nevertheless, in this exercise, it must be cast down and covered over with a cloud of forgetting. You are to step above it stalwartly but lovingly.
>
> (ch. 6)

Even regarding such staples of the Christian spiritual life as meditations on sin and on the "passion, the kindness, and the great goodness and worthiness of God," contemplatives are to "put them down and hold them far under the cloud of forgetting" (ch. 7). No matter how truthful or pious a thought or image or object is, it is to be lovingly but firmly put under foot as a distraction from the experience of that which is beyond all words and images and forms.

This is not to suggest that the ordinary practices of religion or our natural affections for people and objects in our ordinary world are to be suppressed or forgotten. "I want you to reckon each thought and each impulse," he writes, "at its proper value" (ch. 9). The author continually stresses the importance of religious practice and writes that it is often appropriate to reflect upon one's life and the world around one. "But in this exercise it profits little or nothing" (ch. 5). In order "to feel and see God as he is in himself" it is necessary to enter "this darkness and this cloud" in which everything else fades into the background.

The cloud of unknowing is not an isolated or momentary "peak experience." It is rather embedded in a practice. Arising out of the disciplines of the spiritual life, the cloud of unknowing itself constitutes a further discipline. "Learn to be at home in this darkness. Return to it as often as you can" – this speaks of a practice, not an episodic event. And there is no surpassing it, no stage beyond it. Even the most experienced adept remains under the cloud of unknowing.

> There never yet existed, nor ever shall be, so pure a creature, one so ravished on high in contemplation and love of the godhead, who did not find this high and wonderful cloud of unknowing between him and his God.
>
> (ch. 17)

Here too there is the process of surrendering to experience that we noted in our discussion of the psychology of religious transformation. Like the Pentecostal surrendering to the baptism of the Holy Spirit or the Tibetan disciples putting themselves into the hands of their master, the practitioner of the *via negativa* surrenders to the black hole into which all their cherished religious formularies and symbols gradually sink. "It is usual to find nothing but a darkness around your mind, or, as it were, a cloud of unknowing. You will know nothing and feel nothing . . . Learn to be at home in this darkness. Return to it as often as you can."

Such a process is far from easy or painless. The contemporary Thomas Merton writes, "If we set out into this darkness, we have to meet these inexorable forces. We will have to face fears and doubts. We will have to call into question the whole structure of our spiritual lives" (Merton, 1973: 96). Later he calls this a process "that risks intolerable purifications, and sometimes, indeed very often, the risk turns out to be too great to be tolerated" (1966: 58). Such states of consciousness are difficult, almost unbearable, for "We do not find it easy to subsist in a void in which our natural powers have nothing of their own to rely on" (1961: 135).

RELIGION WITHOUT IDEALIZATION

Merton strikes a cord that is little heard in the classical literature: the theme of loss and mourning. Classical texts like Dionysius and *The Cloud* emphasize more the transformation that results from the *via negativa* and say very little about the experience of loss and a concomitant period of mourning. For them the *via negativa* is gain much more than loss. But for Merton, who was certainly knowledgeable about psychoanalysis, the apophatic way entails loss, and loss is automatically connected to mourning.

For Freud, loss leads to mourning and mourning involves internalizing the lost object in order to sustain the attachment to it. The lost object is preserved by being taken inside the self: the connection is maintained, except now it is to an internalized object rather than an external one. An external object (usually a person who has died) now becomes a psychological structure. Thus a new, internal aspect of the personality is created out of the experience of loss. In the case of Merton, then, the *via negativa* can be understood as the transformation of lost objects of belief into a more internalized and diffuse sense of the divine. However, in the classical texts like *The Cloud* the traditional objects of belief are not lost or given up, only put in a new context.

The *via negativa* begins from and returns to the ordinary routines of a religious tradition: its beliefs, texts, rituals, and symbols. Gradually, after a time of living and working with them, these forms begin to lose their former profundity. Not because of secularization or some intellectual critique of religion, for this process occurred to people long before the advent of modernity. Rather because the religious practitioner is coming to the limits of any finite form in the face of the ultimate. Thus the *via negativa* arises out of traditional religious practices taken to their limit.

Psychologically the *via negativa* involves the willingness to go beyond these forms – often driven beyond them by the trajectory of experience – into the void. But the forms are not simply outgrown or left behind as though this was a normal process of psychological development or a program of philosophical critique and rejection. For example, in the tradition of Christian spirituality, monks and other contemplatives continue to read scripture, chant, and pray. The lamas of Tibet still engage in regular monastic ritual practices. The author of *The Cloud of Unknowing* insists that his reader continue in the regular practices of the Christian church even while moving beyond them (ch. 35).

Instead of being rejected or outgrown, the quotidian forms of religion – the creeds, texts, symbols, and rituals – are repositioned in a larger context. No longer sacred ends in themselves, they are now embraced as means to a greater end, what the desert fathers in Christianity called "pure prayer" or "imageless prayer," in other words, the cloud of unknowing wherein God is known as God by not being known (in a conventional sense) at all.

A dialectical relationship is established between the experience of God as void and abyss and the forms and structures of daily religious commitment. In entering the cloud of unknowing, the spiritual seeker goes beyond the forms – casting them down and covering them over with a cloud of forgetting, stepping above them stalwartly but lovingly (ch. 6). While no longer identified with the divine reality, which is beyond all possible identifications, prayers and texts and symbols are still valued as part of the larger context of practice in which the spiritual seeker lives.

Thus the *via negativa* de-idealizes the forms of religion. Not in the sense of Max Weber's disenchantment in which religious forms are debunked, rejected, or outgrown, which is the type of religious de-idealization represented by Freud and classical psychoanalysis. Rather they are de-idealized in the sense that the sacred status of all religious forms is relativized. Thus the *via negativa* represents a form of religious de-idealization very different from that carried by classical analysis with its Enlightenment faith in the vanquishing of religion by science. Classical psychoanalysts and their modern counterparts, like most nineteenth-century critics of religion, assumed that the only possibilities left for religion in the modern world were a skeptical disenchantment in which religion was to be replaced by psychoanalytic insight, or defensively holding onto a naive and superstitious faith, or an abstract and overly intellectualized substitute for religion by those whom Freud ridiculed as thinking "they can rescue the God of religion by replacing him by an impersonal, shadowy and abstract principle" (1962: 21). The *via negativa* offers a modality of de-idealization that is an alternative to the skeptical rejection of religion, or naive superstition, or a lifeless abstraction, and it cannot be equated with any of them.

Here my interpretation of the process of de-idealization supplements that set forth by Peter Homans in his monumental work *The Ability to Mourn: Disillusionment and the Social Origins of Psychoanalysis*. Tracing in great detail the lives and works of Freud, Jung, Weber, and others of that same European intellectual cohort, Homans discerns a pattern that begins with their critique and rejection of religion and other inherited cultural meaning systems in which they were raised. This drives them into a period of mourning in which the person, cut loose from communal systems of meaning, turns inward to confront his own internal processes. This turn inward makes possible a process Homans calls individuation (a Jungian term given a new meaning), which can give rise to new, more psychologically informed, ways of making meaning that, nevertheless, retain some reconfigured ties to the individual's religious and cultural past. Although he does not say so directly, Homans seems to imply that this is the only course that religious de-idealization can take.

Using the example of *The Cloud of Unknowing* and other apophatic writers like Merton, I am suggesting another possible trajectory of de-idealization besides that laid out by Homans and, before him, by Weber. Surrendering to the experience of de-idealization and entering the void can also lead the individual to a renewed and transformed religious sensibility and practice that can still contain the now de-idealized symbols and forms. Thus de-idealization can lead to renewed religious transformation as well as to skeptical disenchantment.

Also this pattern of de-idealization leading inevitably to a skeptical disenchantment certainly fits the figures, all late nineteenth-century European intellectuals, about whom Homans writes. It also mirrors the trajectory of secularization in European society as a whole. And the generalization of this pattern of skeptical disenchantment beyond that rather limited cohort of European intellectuals mirrors the generalization of Weber's thesis of disenchantment and secularization beyond northern European societies to all societies. However, this generalization of the process of secularization to societies beyond northern Europe has been subject to severe criticism lately (Berger, 1999). I am suggesting that just as the European process of secularization may not be followed by all societies as they enter the modern world, so the skeptical disenchantment of religion may not be the only path followed by individuals as they move through a process in which their formerly idealized religious beliefs are de-idealized.

However, no religion can only live out of the apophatic tradition. The Christian gospel proclaims in its doctrine of the Trinity that from the divine abyss flows love. Mahayana Buddhism declares that Sunyata ("emptiness") expresses itself as wisdom and compassion. The void, by itself, is not a religious object but rather gives rise to the objects of idealization which men and women call upon as sacred.

Beyond the categories of emptiness and fullness, in the apophatic tradition the divine reality is not a vacuum. She expresses herself through a variety of images without being identical with them. The speculations of the Upanishads and the image of the drop of water vanishing into the sea, the koans of Zen Buddhism and the lure of paradox, the heroics of Camus and Sartre, the soaring calculations of Einstein whose God does not play dice, the grace of Jesus who forgives us our trespasses, the love of the Great Mother whose wisdom is read on the wind – all are permutations of the presence of the void.

In ordinary language the phrase "presence of the void" makes no sense, since we think that a void is what is absent, not present. But if the "present void" were only an empty absence, experiences of the void could not be empowering. Nor could they clothe themselves in the love of Jesus, the denunciations of Isaiah, the compassion of the ten thousand Bodhisattvas, or the wisdom of the Great Mother. The encounter with the "presence of the void" is never simply negation or despair.

The experience of emptiness is not itself empty. It is overflowing, leaving in its wake the seeds of wisdom and the power of the spirit. Such encounters are not grist for speculative mills; rather in returning to them again and again, people learn to dance and sing, become empowered, and grow in wisdom.

The apophatic trajectory serves to de-idealize or keep in check the idealizing tendencies that can erupt whenever the divine reality is spoken of too directly or any finite institution, writing, structure, or experience is linked too closely to the divine existence. But it also grounds those same de-idealized or relativized religious objects in a transcendental source. The *via negativa* de-idealizes the sacred objects of devotion at the core of every religion and simultaneously connects them to a universal wellspring. It represents one possibility for a vital religion without idealization.

Epilogue

Psychology in general and psychoanalysis in particular are often associated with the rejection of religion. This book demonstrates that a more complex approach to religion exists within contemporary psychoanalytic thinking. Going beyond Hartmann's (1960) suggestion that religion can perform generally supportive and adaptive roles by providing moral guidance, social support, and the transmission of cultural wisdom, several contemporary psychoanalytic theorists imply that religion can make its own unique contribution to mental health and personal transformation.

D. W. Winnicott proposes a "transitional" sphere of knowledge, neither purely objective nor subjective, that is the source of vitality and creativity and is necessary for the "fully human life." Here the tension between objectivity and subjectivity is temporarily overcome in an experience "which expands into creative living and into the whole cultural life of man . . . It is here that the individual experiences creative living" (1971: 102–3). Such moments of rapture and ecstasy are necessary for psychological rejuvenation and sanity. In the pursuit of this richness of consciousness, religious practices can facilitate this transforming psychological space from which renewal and creativity emerge. Rituals, words, stories, and introspective disciplines provide entrance into transitional psychological spaces that are pregnant with the possibility of intuition and transformation.

Christopher Bollas and Emmanuel Ghent elaborate different aspects of Winnicott's theorizing that have immediate relevance for seeing religion in a new light. Bollas's "transformational object," which recapitulates the primal psychological experiences of birth and rebirth, has direct resonances with the encounter with the sacred, an encounter that is often transformative individually and socially. Bollas acknowledges that such "transformational objects" are often denoted as "sacred" because of their power to transfigure an individual's life and that such encounters can have immensely positive results.

Ghent's distinction between submission and surrender nuances the claim, going back to Freud and given forceful expression by Fromm, that religion requires a masochistic submission to authority. In many cases that may be true. But Ghent points out that there can also be a liberating form of surrender in which the grip of the false self is broken and the true self freed. Religious devotion has often presented examples of self-destructive submission, but it can also provide a powerful context in which a liberating surrender can safely take place.

Hans Loewald reframes the dynamic unconscious into the internal ground of the experience of timelessness and unity. He articulates a vision of human life characterized by an ongoing, continual mutual interpenetration between levels of the mind, conscious and unconscious, ego and id. Not antagonists, these different states of awareness are rather different ways of knowing, for "the undifferentiating unconscious is a genuine form of mentation" (1978: 64–5). Loewald provides psychoanalysis with a very rich, complex, and non-reductive understanding of mental life. Conscious rationality alone "limits and impoverishes" our existence unless it has access to the more unitive and intuitive forms of knowing grounded in the dynamic unconscious. The primary process with its complementary forms of rationality must be accessible even to the most highly developed intellect, for sanity requires not the renunciation of the primary process but rather openness to it. Ordinary rationality arises out from but must remain in contact with its source in the dynamic unconscious. Religious experience can keep us open to ways of knowing and being rooted in the primary process with its unitary and timeless sensibility. Loewald speaks psychoanalytically of the timeless, spaceless, unitary ground of existence, beyond language, from which the individual emerges and to which she returns. This ground of existence cannot be spoken of or known about in a subject–object way. But it can be experienced in mystical states that go beyond the subject–object dichotomy.

Kohut calls for "a new religion which is capable of fortifying man's love for its old and new ideals." This religion will enable individuals to transcend their egoism in order to participate "in a supraindividual and timeless existence" (1978a: 456) in which the person is joined to a "supraordinate Self." By feeling connected to a larger and more encompassing (sacred?) reality, individual self-centeredness is de-centered and relocated in a greater, "cosmic" context. Such a "transformation of narcissism into the spirit of religiosity" appears to require moving beyond "the voice of the intellect" to the formulation of "an as yet uncreated system of mystical rationality"(Kohut, 1985: 70). Such an "amalgamation [of psychoanalysis] with mystical modes of thinking" (1985: 71) points to the development of something analogous to a spiritual practice built upon "a constructive mysticism" (1985: 71).

For these contemporary psychoanalysts, religion does not simply play a supportive role in mental health by providing guidance, coping skills, and social support, although it may do all those things. Nor is it primarily an aesthetic supplement to rational living. For Loewald and Winnicott religious experience gives us an authentic knowledge of reality. For Loewald religious experience is a way of knowing ourselves and the world under the rubric of unity and timelessness. For Winnicott it is a way of knowing that gets beyond the dichotomy of subjectivity and objectivity. For both, religious experience enables us to enter a state of awareness from which creative insights and intuitions arise. For Loewald, and apparently for Kohut, reason itself must be transformed by a religious discipline that continually reconnects it with the dynamic unconscious and the forms of knowing found there or expands its narcissistic roots into a more cosmic orientation. This is part and parcel of the critique, by contemporary psychoanalysis, of the rationalistic ideal which dominated earlier psychoanalytic thinking, that sanity is equivalent to the hegemony of technical reason. Rather, what Winnicott calls "the fully human life" requires access to a variety of states of awareness and an ongoing process of personal transformation.

From this psychological perspective, this book has traced two interrelated questions: What is the nature of religion, and how might we understand its capacity to sponsor both lofty ideals and horrific deeds?

At the heart of living religion is the idealization of certain everyday objects – books, ideas, natural sites, teachers, and so forth. The capacity to idealize is not necessarily pathological (although it can be, as described by Freud, Fairbairn, Klein, Fromm, and others) but may represent a healthy state of self-cohesion. As Kohut says quite explicitly, religion exists in continuity with other healthy forms of idealization such as are found in art, literature, and romance. Such idealizations provide much of the transforming power of religious experience. Transformation and self-cohesion are among the potentially positive contributions of religious idealizations to the psychological life.

On the other hand, idealization can contribute to the infantilization of religious devotees, by keeping them in a state of object hunger, as well as to religious fanaticism. These are two of the destructive results of religious idealizations. So we are left with this essential paradox of the powerfully positive and the horrendously destructive results of religious idealization – the paradox of terror and transformation.

So we return at the end to the question raised at the beginning – Is it possible to have a religion without idealization? Is it possible to have both the concrete objects of devotion – the texts, teachers, buildings, natural wonders – the idealization of which makes for lived religion and the critical, prophetic, or apophatic drive which hopefully precludes religious fanaticism? In other words, can one idealize and de-idealize the same religious object at the same time?

Apophatic mysticism provides one example, found in many major religious traditions, of religion in which idealization is chastened and kept in bounds. We might also continue the earlier analogy with romantic love. Kohut described a dialectic between idealization and realism in romantic love. Can I let myself totally idealize my beloved and yet also know that this is romance, this is idealization, that no-one else sees my beloved in the way that I do, but no-one else knows her as I do too. Idealization keeps emotional investment high and passion intense. Realism keeps desires and expectations within the realm of the possible.

Is the same dialectic possible in the religious realm? Can religious idealization be balanced with realistic appraisal: enough idealization to make commitment and transformation possible; enough realism to recognize the limitations and failings of any tradition and so mute fanaticism and keep religiously motivated demands and hopes within the realm of the possible.

Those whose idealizations drive them to confuse fanaticism with devotion may find such a nuanced approach to religious commitment or romantic love impossible. But when splitting and the "moral defense" have been put aside, than the possibility of a balance within religion between realism and idealization opens up.

This requires both a religious and a psychological transformation of the kind hinted at by Kohut with his suggestion of a "cosmic narcissism" and by Loewald in his advocacy of a more complex and transformative way of knowing. Gone is any notion (like that found in Durkheim and Otto) of the holy as an overpowering and coercive force that evokes a "moral defense" in which we are tempted to debase ourselves in order to idealize another. Instead there is, implicitly or explicitly, a vision of God, like that found in *The Cloud of Unknowing*, as an object of desire. The necessity of splitting is thereby lessened, creating an opportunity for a more complex religious experience in which transformation might take place without either infantilization or terror against the self and others.

References

Allport, G. (1962). *The Individual and His Religion.* New York: Macmillan.

Altemeyer, B. and Hunsberger, B. (1992). Authoritarianism, Religious Fundamentalism, Quest, and Prejudice. *International Journal for the Psychology of Religion* 2/2: 113–34.

Ammerman, N. (1994). Accounting for Christian Fundamentalisms. In M. Marty and R. Appleby, *Accounting for Fundamentalisms.* Chicago: University of Chicago Press.

Aran, G. (1991). Jewish Zionist Fundamentalism. In M. Marty and R. Appleby, *Fundamentalisms Observed.* Chicago: University of Chicago Press, pp. 265–344.

Arbib, M. and Hesse, M. (1986). *The Construction of Reality.* Cambridge: Cambridge University Press.

Berg, D. (1997). Pluralism, Religious Bias and Pathologizing. A dissertation submitted to the University of Ottawa.

Berger, P. (1999). *The Desecularization of the World.* Grand Rapids: Eerdmans.

Bollas, C. (1987). *The Shadow of the Object.* New York: Columbia University Press

Browning, D. (1975). *Generative Man.* New York: Delta-Dell.

Capps, D. (1997). *Men, Religion and Melancholia: James, Otto, Jung, and Erikson.* New Haven: Yale University Press.

Chodorow, N. (1989). *Feminism and Psychoanalytic Theory.* New Haven: Yale University Press.

Chodorow, N. (1999). *The Power of Feelings.* New Haven: Yale University Press.

The Cloud of Unknowing (1973). Ed. W. Johnston. New York: Doubleday.

The Cloud of Unknowing (1981). Ed. J. Walsh. New York: Paulist Press.

Covington, D. (1995). *Salvation on Sand Mountain.* New York: Penguin.

Cunningham, L., Kelsey, J., Barineau, R., McVoy, H. (1992). *The Sacred Quest: An Invitation to the Study of Religion.* New York: Macmillan.

Don-Yehiya, E. (1994) The Book and the Sword: The Nationalist Yeshivot and Political Radicalism in Israel. In M. Marty and R. Appleby, *Accounting for Fundamentalisms*. Chicago: University of Chicago Press.

Durkheim, E. (1965). *The Elementary Forms of the Religious Life*, trans. J. Swain. New York: Free Press.

Eliade, M. (1961). *The Sacred and the Profane*. New York: Harper & Row.

Fairbairn, W. R. D. (1952). The Repression and Return of Bad Objects. In *Psychoanalytic Studies of the Personality*. London: Tavistock.

Finn, M. (1992). Transitional Space and Tibetan Buddhism: The Object Relations of Meditation. In M. Finn, and J. Gartner, *Object Relations Theory and Religion*. Westport: Praeger.

Flax, J. (1990). *Thinking Fragments: Psychoanalysis, Feminism and Postmodernism*. Berkeley: University of California Press.

Fowler, J. (1987). *Faith Development and Pastoral care*. Philadelphia: Fortress.

Freud, S. (1914). On Narcissism: An introduction. *Standard Edition*, 14, pp. 73–102.

Freud, S. (1950). *Totem and Taboo*. New York: Norton.

Freud, S. (1962). *Civilization and its Discontents*. New York: Norton.

Freud, S. (1964). *The Future of an Illusion*. Garden City: Doubleday Anchor.

Fromm, E. (1947). *Man for Himself*. New York: Fawcett Publications.

Fromm, E. (1950). *Psychoanalysis and Religion*. New Haven: Yale University Press.

Funk, M. (1998). *A Mind at Peace*. Oxford: Lion.

Galanter, M. (1989). *Cults*. NY: Oxford University Press.

Ghent, E. (1990). Masochism, Submission, and Surrender. *Contemporary Psychoanalysis* 24: 108–36.

Gold, D. (1991). Organized Hinduisms: From Vedic Truth to Hindu Nation. In M. Marty and R. Appleby, *Fundamentalisms Observed*. Chicago: University of Chicago Press.

Gorday, P. (2000). The Self Psychology of Heinz Kohut: What's it all about Theologically? *Pastoral Psychology* 48/6: 445–68.

Gorsuch, R. (1995). Religious Aspects of Substance Abuse and Recovery. *Journal of Social Issues* 5: 65–83.

Greenberg, J. and Mitchell, S. (1983). *Object Relations in Psychoanalytic Theory*. Cambridge: Harvard University Press.

Happold, F. (1975). *Mysticism*. New York: Penguin.

Hartmann, H. (1958). *Ego Psychology and the Problem of Adaption*. New York: International Universities Press.

Hartmann, H. (1960). *Psychoanalysis and Moral Values*. New York: International Universities Press.

Hedayat-Diba, Z. (1997). Selfobject Functions of the Koran. *International Journal for the Psychology of Religion* 7: 211–36.

Homans, P. (1989). *The Ability to Mourn: Disillusionment and the Social Origins of Psychoanalysis*. Chicago: University of Chicago Press.

James, W. (1982). *The Varieties of Religious Experience*. First published 1902. New York: Penguin.

John of the Cross (1961). *Spiritual Canticle*, trans. E. A. Peers. New York: Doubleday Image.

Jones, J. (1971). Reflections on the Problem of Religious Experience. *Journal of the American Academy of Religion* 40: 445–53.

Jones, J. (1982). The Delicate Dialectic: Religion and Psychology in the Modern World. *Cross Currents*, 32: 143–53.

Jones, J. (1991). *Contemporary Psychoanalysis and Religion*. New Haven: Yale University Press.

Jones, J. (1992). Knowledge in Transition: Toward a Winnicottian Epistemology. *Psychoanalytic Review* 79: 223–37.

Jones, J. (1995). *In the Middle of This Road We Call Our Life*. San Francisco: HarperCollins.

Jones, J. (1996). *Religion and Psychology in Transition: Psychoanalysis, Feminism, and Theology*. New Haven: Yale University Press.

Jones, J. (1997a). The Real is the Relational: Relational Psychoanalysis as a Model of Human Understanding. In J. Belzen (ed.), *Hermeneutical Approaches in the Psychology of Religion*. Atlanta and Amsterdam: Rodopi.

Jones, J. (1997b). Playing and Believing: The Uses of D. W. Winnicott in the Psychology of Religion. In J. Jacobs and D. Capps (eds), *Religion, Society and Psychoanalysis*. Denver: Westview.

Jones, J. (1999). Religion and Psychology in Transition: How it came to be Written; and, Response to Critics. *Pastoral Psychology* 97: 157–64, 183–90.

Jonte-Pace, D. (1992). Situating Kristeva Differently. In D. Crownfield (ed.), *Body/Text in Julia Kristeva: Religion, Women, and Psychoanalysis*. Albany: SUNY Press.

Jonte-Pace, D. (1997). Julia Kristeva and the Psychoanalytic Study of Religion. In J. Jacobs and D. Capps (eds), *Religion, Society and Psychoanalysis*. Denver: Westview.

Jonte-Pace, D. (1999). In Defense of an Unfriendly Freud: Psychoanalysis, Feminism, and Religion. *Pastoral Psychology* 97: 175–82.

Julian, R. (1992). Building Bridges: Teresa of Avila and Self Psychology. *Pastoral Psychology* 41/2: 89–96.

Jung, C. (1938). *Psychology and Religion*. New Haven: Yale University Press.

Kirkpatrick, L., Hood, R., Hartz, G. (1991). Fundamentalist Religion Conceptualized in Terms of Rokeach's Theory of the Open and Closed Mind. *Research in the Social Scientific Study of Religion* 3: 157–79.

Klein, M. (1975a). *Love, Guilt and Reparation, 1921–1945*. New York: Free Press.

Klein, M. (1975b). *Envy and Gratitude, 1946–1963*. New York: Dell.
Kohlberg, L. (1981). Moral Development, Religious Thinking, and the Question of a Seventh Stage. With C. Power, *The Philosophy of Moral Development*, vol. i. New York: Harper & Row.
Kohut, H. (1971). *The Analysis of the Self*. New York: International Universities Press.
Kohut, H. (1978a). Forms and Transformations of Narcissism. In P. Ornstein (ed.), *The Search for the Self*, vol. i, pp. 427–60. New York: International Universities Press.
Kohut, H. (1978b). Remarks about the Formation of the Self. In P. Ornstein (ed.), *The Search for the Self*, vol. ii, pp. 737–70. New York: International Universities Press.
Kohut, H. (1884). *How Does Analysis Cure?* Chicago: University of Chicago Press.
Kohut, H. (1985). *Self Psychology and the Humanities*, ed. C. Strozier. New York: Norton.
Kripal, J. (1998). *Kali's Child*. Chicago: University of Chicago Press.
Kristeva, J. (1987). *In the Beginning was Love: Psychoanalysis and Faith*, trans. A. Goldhammer. New York: Columbia University Press.
Lakoff, G. and Johnson, M. (1980). *Metaphors We Live By*. Chicago: University of Chicago Press.
Lawrence, B. (1989). *Defenders of God*. San Francisco: Harper & Row.
Leavy, S. (1988). *In the Image of God*. New Haven: Yale University Press.
Leech, K. (1985). *Experiencing God*. New York: Harper & Row.
Lichtenberg, J. (1991). What is a Selfobject? *Psychoanalytic Dialogues* 1: 455–79.
Loewald, H. (1980). *Psychoanalysis and the History of the Individual*. New Haven: Yale University Press.
Loewald, H. (1979). *Papers on Psychoanalysis*. New Haven: Yale University Press.
Loewald, H. (1988). *Sublimation*. New Haven: Yale University Press.
Lutzky, H. (1991). The Sacred and the Maternal Object. In H. Siegel (ed.), *Psychoanalytic Reflections on Current Issues*. New York: New York University Press.
Marty, M. and Appleby, R. (1991). *Fundamentalisms Observed*. Chicago: University of Chicago Press.
Marty, M. and Appleby, R. (1994). *Accounting for Fundamentalisms*. Chicago: University of Chicago Press.
Meissner, W. (1984). *Psychoanalysis and Religious Experience*. New Haven: Yale University Press.
Merkur, D. (1992). Spirit and the Problem of Social Instincts: Exceptions to Freud's Critique of Religion. In L. Boyer and R. Boyer (eds), *The Psychoanalytic Study of Society*, vol. xvii. Hillsdale: Analytic Press.

Merton, T. (1961). *New Seeds of Contemplation.* New York: New Directions.
Merton, T. (1966). *Conjectures of a Guilty Bystander.* Garden City: Doubleday Publishers.
Merton, T. (1973). *Contemplative Prayer.* London: Darton, Longman Todd.
Miller-McLemore, B. (1999). The Ontological Status of God and Other Small Questions. *Pastoral Psychology* 97: 165–74.
Mitchell, S. (1993). *Hope and Dread in Psychoanalysis.* New York: Basic Books.
Mitchell, S. (1997). Psychoanalysis and the Degradation of Romance. *Psychoanalytic Dialogues* 7: 23–42.
Mitchell, S. (1998). From Ghosts to Ancestors: The Psychoanalytic Vision of Hans Loewald. *Psychoanalytic Dialogues* 8/6: 825–56.
Niebuhr, R. (1932). *Moral Man and Immoral Society.* New York: Charles Scribner's Sons.
Ornstein, P. (1998). Heinz Kohut's Vision. In P. Marcus and A. Rosenberg (eds), *Psychoanalytic Visions of the Human Condition.* New York: New York University Press.
Otto, R. (1958). *The Idea of the Holy*, trans. J. W. Harvey. New York: Oxford University Press.
Parsons, W. (1999). *The Enigma of the Oceanic Feeling.* New York: Oxford University Press.
Piscatori, J. (1994). Accounting for Islamic Fundamentalisms. In M. Marty and R. Appleby, *Accounting for Fundamentalisms.* Chicago: University of Chicago Press.
Proudfoot, W. (1985). *Religious Experience.* Berkeley: University of California Press.
Pruyser, P. (1968). *A Dynamic Psychology of Religion.* New York: Harper & Row.
Pruyser, P. (1983). *The Play of the Imagination: Toward a Psychoanalysis of Culture.* New York: International Universities Press.
Rambo, R. (1993). *Understanding Religious Conversion.* New Haven: Yale University Press.
Randall, R. (1980). Soteriological Dimensions in the Work of Heinz Kohut. *Journal of Religion and Health* 19/2: 83–91.
Randall, R. (1984). The Legacy of Kohut for Religion and Psychology. *Journal of Religion and Health* 23/2: 106–14.
Randall, R. (nd). Religion within the Framework of Self Psychology. Unpublished paper.
Rinpoche, Sogyal (1992). *The Tibetan Book of Living and Dying.* New York: HarperCollins.
Ritter, K. and O'Neill, C. (1996). *Righteous Religion.* New York: Haworth Press.

Rizzuto, A. M. (1979). *The Birth of the Living God*. Chicago: University of Chicago Press.

Rubin, J. (1996). *Psychotherapy and Buddhism*. New York: Plenum.

Schmidt, R. (1998). *Exploring Religion*. Belmont, CA: Wadsworth Publishing Co.

Selengut, C. (1994). By Torah Alone: Yeshiva Fundamentalism in Jewish Life. In M. Marty and R. Appleby, *Accounting for Fundamentalisms*. Chicago: University of Chicago Press.

Shafranske, E. (1992). God Representations as the Transformational Object. In M. Finn and J. Gartner, *Object Relations Theory and Religion*. Westport: Praeger.

Smart, N. (1996). *Dimensions of the Sacred*. Berkeley: University of California Press.

Strozier, C. (1994). *Apocalypse: On the Psychology of Fundamentalism in America*. Boston: Beacon.

Strozier, C. (1997). Heinz Kohut's Struggles with Religion, Ethnicity, and God. In J. Jacobs and D. Capps (eds), *Religion, Society, and Psychoanalysis*. Boulder: Westview.

Swearer, D. (1991). Fundamentalist Movements in Theravada Buddhism. In M. Marty and R. Appleby, *Fundamentalisms Observed*. Chicago: University of Chicago Press.

Tillich, P. (1957). *Dynamics of Faith*. New York: Harper & Row.

Turner, V. (1967) *The Forest of Symbols*. Ithaca: Cornell University Press.

Turner, V. (1969). *The Ritual Process*. Ithaca: Cornell University Press.

Turner, V. (1986). Body, Brain, and Culture. *Cross Currents* 36: 156–78.

Winnicott, D. W. (1965). *The Maturational Process and the Facilitating Environment*. London: Hogarth.

Winnicott, D. W. (1971). *Playing and Reality*. New York: Routledge.

Woo, R. and Mannes, J. (1997). A Psychological and Psychoanalytical Response to "Selfobject Functions of the Koran." *International Journal for the Psychology of Religion* 7: 241–4.

Wulff, D. (1991). *Psychology of Religion*. New York: John Wiley.

Index